9 Steps To Achieve Your Destiny

Do your best and let the Creator take care of the rest!

Zohra Sarwari

EMAN
publishing

Cover Design by Zeeshan Shaikh

Printed in the United States of America

9 Steps To Achieve Your Destiny

Do your best and let the Creator take care of the rest!

Zohra Sarwari

Dedication

'(Our Lord! Accept this from us; You are the All-Hearing, the All-Knowing).'

(The Qur'aan: Chapter 2, Verse 127)

Acknowledgments

In the name of the Allaah, the Most Gracious, the Most Magnificent. All praise is due to Allaah, Lord of the universe. We praise Him, and seek His help and His forgiveness, and we seek His protection from the accursed Satan. Whomever Allaah guides will never be misguided, and whomever He allows to be misguided will never be guided. I bear witness that there is no deity worthy of worship except Allaah, who is One; alone, and has no partners. I bear witness that Muhammad is His servant and messenger. May the blessings of Allaah be upon him, his family, his companions, and the righteous that follow them, until the Day of Judgment.

I would like to thank my family and friends for all of their support, especially Zeeshan, Madeeha, and Saqib Sheikh, who are an asset to my team *masha'Allaah*. A very special thanks goes to Dr. Daoud Nassimi for all of his efforts and hard work in editing this book – *jazaakum-Allaahu khayran* - May Allaah (SWT) reward you all - *ameen!*

Terminology

1. **"ALLAAH"** is the Arabic name for THE ONE SUPREME UNIVERSAL GOD.
2. **"SWT"** is an abbreviation of the Arabic words *"Subhaanahu wa Ta'ala"* which means "Glory Be To Him".
3. **Al-Qur'aan:** The Book of Allaah; divine guidance for mankind; the FINAL TESTAMENT.
4. **Muslim** is one who has submitted to the Will of ALLAAH.
5. **Allaahu-Akbar** means ALLAAH is the Greatest.
6. **Assalaamu-alaykum** means 'Peace be upon you.' It is a greeting among the Muslims. The response to this greeting is 'Wa 'alaykum assalaam,' which means 'And Peace be upon you'.
7. **Hajj** is one of the five pillars of Islam, a duty one must perform during one's life-time if one has the financial resources for it. It must be performed during certain specified dates of Dhul-Hijjah.
8. **PBUH** means Peace Be Upon Him.
9. **PBUT** means Peace Be Upon Them.
10. **Alhamdulillaah** means Praise be to God!
11. **Jazaak Allaahu khayran** means 'May Allaah reward you with good'.
12. **5 Daily Prayers:**
    1. *__Fajr (pre-dawn):__* This prayer starts off the day with the remembrance of Allaah (SWT); it is performed before sunrise.
    2. *__Dhuhr (noon):__* After the day's work has begun, one breaks shortly after noon to again remember Allaah (SWT) and seek His guidance.
    3. *__'Asr (afternoon):__* In the late afternoon, people are usually busy wrapping up the day's work, getting kids home from school, etc. It is an important time to take a few minutes to remember Allaah (SWT) and the greater meaning of our lives.
    4. *__Maghrib (sunset):__* Just after the sun goes down, Muslims remember Allaah (SWT) again as the day comes to a close.
    5. *__'Isha (evening):__* Before retiring for the night, Muslims again take time to remember Allaah (SWT)'s presence, guidance, mercy, and forgiveness.
13. **Adhaan** is the call to Prayer.

14. **Du'aa** is supplication in Islam.

15. **Insha'Allaah** means 'If Allaah wills'.

16. **Hadith** means the actions and sayings of Prophet Muhammad (PBUH), reported by his companions, and collected by scholars who came after them, in books.

17. **Tahajjud** is a voluntary prayer read in the last part of the night. It is also known as 'qiyaam'.

18. **Subhaan'Allaah** means "Glory to Allaah".

19. **Takbeer** is the saying of 'Allaahu Akbar.'

20. **Sunnah** means the deeds, sayings and approvals of Muhammad (PBUH).

21. **Sahaabah** means Companions of the Prophet Muhammad (PBUH).

22. **Deen** means Religion.

23. **Dunya** means the world.

24. **Surah** refers to a chapter in Qur'aan.

Table of Contents

Step 1:

The Power of Reading

"Wali, aren't you done with the book yet?"

"Not yet," Wali answered his sister.

"Hurry up, can't you?" Zeba said. "I want to read it too." "Just a little longer, I promise." Wali sighed. He and his sister were the first in their family to learn to read English. Nancy, their next-door neighbor, was a retired English teacher. Though the family could only afford to pay her for lessons once a week, Nancy actually came twice each week, delighted with the eagerness of the brother and sister to learn, and with how quickly they mastered the lessons. No one had to remind them to study or do homework — it was something both had taken to with genuine enthusiasm.

Whenever the family was able to get hold of a book, Wali grabbed it to read first. He had a dream that so far he had shared with no one; that one day he would have a large library of books, all kinds of books; and, he would be reading them, his children would know so much more in turn than he did.

In Afghanistan, before they had come to America as refugees, his family had been well-to-do. They had lived in comfort, with servants to care for their needs. It broke Wali's heart to see how hard both his parents had to work just to support themselves and their two children, and their grandparents.

The more he had thought about it, the more certain he became that the poverty in which they lived now was a result of the poverty of their education — neither his parents nor his grandparents had any real education. Wali had vowed, though, that he would not perpetuate that poverty. He thanked Allaah (SWT), God the Greatest, for all that he had, but he fervently wanted to do more with his life than his parents and grandparents had done with theirs.

He was convinced that the secret to doing so was to break the cycle of illiteracy that had shackled his family for generations. That was his greatest dream, but how he was to accomplish that, he had no idea. In his heart, he was sure there was a way, and he believed that this conviction, too, was a gift from Allaah (SWT), but he had no idea where the path to his goals lay. How was he to find it?

Money wasn't everything, he knew that, but without it, he and Zeba would not be able to go to college. Their father was no longer a young man. The time would come when he would be unable to support the family. Someone else would have to care for them and pay the bills. Without proper education, how were he and Zeba to look after their parents and grandparents when that time came, let alone raise their own children.

Zeba, waiting with barely restrained impatience in the chair across the table from him, took a deep breath. "Is the book interesting?" she asked.

"Yes."

"What have you learned?"

"Many things," he said, barely taking his eyes from the printed page. "I'm learning how I can go to the proper schools and make money, so that I will be able to take care of all of us in time."

As he said this, Wali's expression was one of grim determination — but there was something else in it as well; his eyes glowed with determination and hope.

> *"Knowledge is useless, if action is not taken."*
> Zohra Sarwari

1   "Reading is a process of retrieving and comprehending some form of stored information or ideas. These ideas are usually some sort of representation of language, such as symbols to be examined by sight, or by touch (for example Braille). Other types of reading may not be text-based, such as music notation or pictograms. By analogy, in computer science, reading is acquiring of data from some sort of computer storage." – www.Wikipedia.org

To watch a child or an adult first read is the most fascinating sight. The excitement and joy is overwhelming. Reading builds confidence. Everyone is able to read, even those who cannot see.

Louis Braille was the founder of the Braille system in 1821. Braille is a binary code, which represents characters of a writing system, and blind people can use this system to communicate through reading and writing.

Usually books tend to fall into two categories, nonfiction and fiction. Nonfiction means the story is true or the person telling the story presumes it's true. Nonfiction includes history, biographies, essays, journals, documentaries, scientific papers, textbooks, blueprints, technical documentation, journalism, and more. Fiction books are stories or novels that are made up. Examples of fiction are comic books, fables, fairy tales, novels, and so on.

Proofreading is the careful reading and editing of a manuscript to ensure it has no typographical or grammatical errors before being published. For example, one writes an essay, and then asks someone to read the guidelines that were given and read the paper to make sure it follows accordingly. Before a book is printed, it must be proofread.

Speed-reading is when one reads at a faster pace. The more one reads and comprehends, the faster he or she can read. An example of this would be my sister. She read lots of books. Everywhere she went as she was growing up she was reading: parties, funerals, parks, weddings, etc. The summer of her eighth grade year she must have read at least 200 books. They weren't small books. After that summer, she continued reading a great deal, and her reading and comprehension were beyond the average eighth grader.

When we began college together, I realized she could understand and comprehend at a much faster rate than I. In college, we took the same classes. She would study two hours before the test and get a B in the class, while I studied for two weeks for the same grade or better. I realized the biggest difference between us was she read much more than I did. It was at that moment I had an epiphany. I realized the power of reading. I began to read more and more, and wanted to become faster at comprehending and reading, so I didn't waste time later. Now, thanks to Allaah (SWT), I read at least four to five books a month, which is only night-time reading; before I go to bed. If I hadn't read a lot when I was younger, I probably wouldn't be able to finish even one book a month.

2 Why do we need to read?

We need to read to have fluency of words, comprehension of language, and to help us become creative thinkers.

Fluency of words means that our vocabulary needs to be expanded and we have all the words we need to be able to express ourselves. According to www.wikipedia.org, the average person retains 10,000 vocabulary words. According to Oxford University Press, the English language has about 600,000 words. That means the percentage of words we use and know is less than 2% of what is out there. If we read more, our vocabulary will expand, and words we didn't previously know will flow from our mouths.

Comprehending languages is a vital part of everyone's life. In today's world, everyone is exposed to a minimum of two languages; which means becoming multilingual is vital to our success. When one understands other languages, he is exposed to other cultures and his vocabulary will grow, making him a better-rounded person.

What does reading have to do with creative thinking? The more one reads the more creative he becomes. Reading takes one to another dimension in thinking. New ideas take time to emerge. The more we allow our minds to imagine, the more we create associations between existing ideas or concepts. For example, once the television was available; creative thinking on the part of others led to the creation of the VCR, DVD, satellite reception and more. All of this happens when minds become creative.

Creativity is the key to success. We have to find the genius in each of us, and only then can we tap into our creativity and discover what Allaah (SWT) has blessed us with.

The next two sections discuss people to whom reading was very important.

3 Who is Prophet Muhammad (Peace Be Upon Him)?

Prophet Muhammad (PBUH) was the last and final messenger sent down by Allaah (SWT), God the Greatest, to bring Islam to the people. Prophet Muhammad (PBUH) was not the creator of a new religion, but the restorer of the original, uncorrupted monotheistic faith of Adam, Abraham (Ibrahim), Noah (Nuh), Moses (Musa), and Jesus (Eisa) (Peace be upon them all). Prophet Muhammad (PBUH) was the last and the greatest in a series of prophets. He (PBUH) was the 'Seal of the Prophets'.

The first revelation that Archangel Jibreel gave the Prophet Muhammad (PBUH) was "Iqra," which means "Read." Prophet Muhammad (PBUH) replied, "I cannot read." The Angel Jibreel (PBUH) then embraced him until he reached the limit of his endurance, and after releasing him said, "Iqra." Prophet Muhammad's (PBUH) answer was the same. Jibreel (PBUH) repeated this a third time, and asked him to repeat after him and said:

"Read in the name of your Lord who created! He created man from that which clings. Read, and thy Lord is most Bountiful, Who taught by the pen, taught man what he knew not."

When I first read those lines and was told of the story, I was blown away. I knew that reading and knowledge were vital to one's success and that education was very important, but I didn't realize that a message from Allaah (SWT) told us to seek knowledge. So I speak to those who believe in God the Greatest, and say that Allaah (SWT) has given us gifts that none of the other creatures in the world possess. It is time we took our gifts and excelled in them by reading about everything. To perfect one, we must find examples of perfection from our communities and other communities, and learn from their examples. Without reading and knowledge, it is very difficult for us to achieve those goals.

There are other important references in Islam about knowledge, such as: *"Seeking knowledge is obligatory upon every Muslim. Allaah will make the path to Paradise easy for one who treads on the path to knowledge. Seek knowledge from the cradle to the grave. Verily the men of knowledge are the inheritors of the Prophets."*

The text of the Qur'aan is filled with verses inviting man to use his intellect, to ponder, to think, and to know, for the goal of human life is to discover the Truth; which is none other than worshipping God in His Oneness.

4 Who are some of the people who have become successful due to reading books?

Anthony Robbins is a rag-to-riches story. Being kicked out of his house at the age of seventeen, he began his first vocation, in sales. He desired personal growth, and within seven years, he had read 700 books. Soon he found himself in the seminar business, selling tickets for a motivational speaker. He broke records in his sales and his income increased. Not long after that, he began his own seminars, and it was around that time his life took on a shape of its own. He now teaches a new therapeutic technique promising to deliver instant transformation by directly altering unconscious "programs." It's a phenomenal way of helping people get over their fears and reach their goals.

Anthony Robbins never went to college, yet he possesses more knowledge than many who have attended school for decades. He is a gifted speaker, an educator, and continues to inspire millions. He has sold more audiotapes worldwide than Michael Jackson, and was a millionaire by the age of 22. Anthony Robbins says, *"I believe life is constantly testing us for our level of commitment, and life's greatest rewards are reserved for those who demonstrate a never-ending commitment to act until they achieve. As simplistic as this may sound, it is still the common denominator separating those who live their dreams from those who live in regret."* (Unknown magazine)

Anthony Robbins is a prime example of someone who was not highly educated, yet READ, and read, and read some more. Through all the knowledge he obtained from reading, he was able to jumpstart his life. It's amazing how one's mind can expand so much from the books read.

Mark Victor Hansen is a motivational speaker and renowned author of the "Chicken Soup for the Soul" series. He is an extraordinary speaker, and has also inspired millions. Most of his success comes back to certain books in his life that changed him forever to make him the man he is today, such as 'As a Man Thinketh', 'Acres of

Diamonds', and 'Think and Grow Rich'. There are many more that have helped him through the hard times. It is books like these that have made him who he is today.

Oprah Winfrey is an Academy Award-nominated actress, an influential book critic, a magazine publisher, and has the highest rated talk show in the history of television. She is also seen as one of the most influential women in the world. Oprah's grandmother taught her how to read before she was three years old. Oprah was always a determined individual and wanted to have success and sacrificed a lot to achieve it. She knew what she wanted, and did everything in her power to achieve it. Today she is the richest African-American woman in the world and has been for three years in a row. She is also a philanthropist, and loves giving to the underprivileged. I feel that her success could be due to many factors, especially the fact that she had a head start on reading. Her mind was spinning a thousand miles per hour at an early age.

It is people like Prophet Muhammad (PBUH), Anthony Robbins, Mark Victor Hansen and Oprah who preach the power of knowledge. The power is within each of us to become a success, if we choose to take that path. However, we all need a little bit of help. Know that reading is a powerful tool and that *"We should seek knowledge from the cradle to the grave."* ---Muslim Scholar. The more one knows, the more one can do. The more one grows, the more one can help society grow. If you want to be the best, you need to know who was the best and learn from the best. Those who achieve excellence in their lives and master themselves didn't do it alone. All of us need to be guided, whether it is spiritually, mentally, physically or financially. We all need to master ourselves, to figure out "What is the purpose of our life?" There is no better time to start than NOW! It's never too early to become great. That's why this book was written — to guide our youth and elders towards achieving greatness in their life, and to become the best humans possible by searching within them; to encourage youth to constantly acquire knowledge, be tolerant of everything that evolves around them, and be wise in how they approach each situation.

My love for reading began when I was young and bored. I realized that books made me imagine things I never knew existed. At some point in my life, I got lazy and didn't read as much, I began watching television instead. I also liked to socialize, and would have fun on the phone. I fell into the belief that TV was cool, like many other teens that have easy access to television. It was after high school and the beginning of college when I realized how smart my sister was because of how much she read. It was then I also had an "aha" moment of how I had wasted my time during my younger years. Things would have been so much easier for me if I had just read thirty minutes a day. I realized the power of reading, and began to read for enjoyment in addition to college reading. It's never too late to start reading.

Alhamdulillaah (All Praise is due to God) that I was able to get back on track with regards to reading, and since then have read hundreds of books for educational and growing purposes. My love for reading only grows more and more with each great book that I read. I learn so many valuable lessons that I just want to read some books over and over. I am amazed at how much I have changed every year due to reading alone.

You can start reading fiction or nonfiction. However, you should read books that will help you become great. If you read thirty minutes five days of the week, in a month that would be 600 minutes, and in a year, 7,200 minutes. In five years that would calculate to 36,000 minutes. Imagine if the books you read were life changing, inspirational, and motivational! What would become of the individual? Only Allaah (SWT), Lord of the universe, knows. He or she might become another Dr. Bilal Philips or Mubarakah Ibrahim. One would be the best of who they are. Imagine if all of this started when one was only seven years old or ten years old. Would that individual be ready to rule the world one day? Would he or she be the hero everyone is looking for? Would that person change the world into a better place because he or she knew the right things to do at the right time?

Ponder these questions and then examine why so many are starting earlier with their children, to build their characters, confidence and values, so they are well-equipped to face the challenges and changes of tomorrow. I believe the books that can totally change an individual are books of Allaah (SWT), God the Greatest, autobiographies and personal development. These three categories are powerful, even for children.

'The Prophet Muhammad (PBUH) said, "Love for humanity what you love for yourself."' - Al-Bukhari

Exercises

The first exercise is to read for ten minutes every evening. Pick books that you enjoy, and then once you've built some momentum, read personal development selections. If it is still too hard for you to begin reading, start reading with a family member, be it a parent, a sibling or someone else living with you. Maybe you can read to them ten minutes every day. If you are successful with the ten minutes- a-day routine, after thirty days, upgrade to twenty minutes a day. Increase your time of reading as you wish, but never go below twenty minutes a day. Make it a habit for yourself. You will see that if you read the right books, you will develop into something extraordinary.

Write down 5 books that you're willing to read.

1. --

2. --

3. --

4. --

5. --

Step 2:

Building Your Character

Finally, after several days, Wali finished reading the book and passed it on to Zeba. The first thing Zeba did was to read the title: 'The Greatest Salesman in the World'.

"But what does that mean?" she asked her brother.

"Once you begin reading, the meaning of the title will make itself clear," he said. The only thing that Wali would tell her was, "The information this book contains is like gold."

Zeba was primarily interested in what this book contained that other books did not. She kept thinking of what Wali had said: "The information this book contains is like gold." She knew that gold was worth a lot, but she couldn't understand how the two could be compared. It dazzled her mind to think this book could make her rich. She quickly finished all her chores that afternoon, grabbed the book, and went to a quiet place to read.

'The Greatest Salesman in the World'; what did "salesman" mean? Wali had said all the answers would be found within the book, so she began reading. She was slow to understand the book at first, as it was a little harder than her usual reading, but Wali had said there was gold in there, and she wanted to discover it.

She knew if she was searching for gold in the real world, she might have to dig deep and hard. She also might have to dig more than one place before she discovered the gold. So, surely the same would be true with finding the treasure in this book. She was willing to be patient and keep reading until she had discovered what Wali had discovered. Within hours she was halfway through the book.

"Zeba," her mother called.

Zeba was so interested in her book that she did not answer immediately.

"Zeba," her mother called again.

As engrossed as she was in the book, Zeba loved her parents deeply and knew that they must come first in her attention. "Just a minute," she said, trying to read just one more page.

Her mother said, "Please come inside and help with preparing dinner."

"Okay, Mom, I will be right there," Zeba said, obediently putting the book aside.

As she went to help her mother, Zeba thought of how fortunate she was. She and Wali had the greatest parents, parents who loved them so much and always tried to teach what was right and wrong. She was very close to her parents and grandparents and she liked being home-schooled. It meant she was able to cook with her mom, help with chores and spend time with her grandparents. Best of all, it meant she could listen to the great stories her parents and grandparents told her about the Prophets (PBUT).

She loved those stories the most. When she was just a little girl, her grandmother had told her of the time when the Prophet Muhammad (PBUH) went one day into the city of Taif to address the people there and invite them to Islam. But the people of Taif and their tribal leaders mocked and ridiculed him and rejected his message. The leaders went so far as to tell everyone, even the children and slaves, to insult him and throw stones at him. The Prophet (PBUH) was stoned until he bled and was forced to leave Taif.

It was then that Allaah (SWT) placed at the Prophet's command the Angel of the Mountains, telling him that the Angel would crush the valley of Taif if he so wished, and slay all the people in the village. But instead of responding to his injuries with anger and vengeance, the Prophet Muhammad (PBUH) only prayed that Allaah (SWT) would help guide them and their offspring toward the right path.

This was one of Zeba's favorite stories and she thought often about the infinite mercy and compassion the Prophet (PBUH) had demonstrated in the face of injustice.

"How is the new book?" her mother asked while they prepared for dinner.

"It's somewhat different from the other books I have read," Zeba replied. "It's harder to understand at first, but I'm not giving up. Wali said that the book was like gold. I must find out where the gold is."

Her mother smiled. "You know," she said, "that is only an expression."

Zeba stopped setting the dinnerware and looked at her mother. "What does that mean?"

"That means it's not really gold, but something that is valued like gold. The information has a lot of value to it, and is probably very useful."

All through dinner Zeba thought about what her mom had said, and about the gold that Wali had promised her the book contained. What lesson would she learn from it that would be of value to her? Although the dinner was delicious, she ate in a rush, eager to get back to her book.

She was in her room again, reading the book and still puzzling over these questions, when her Grandmother came by.

"Zeba, what are you thinking so hard about?" Grandmother asked.

"The new book I'm reading."

Her grandmother said, wistfully, "I wish I had learned to read."

Zeba looked at her grandmother's surprisingly youthful face. She had only a few wrinkles by her eyes and on her forehead to indicate the years she had lived. How beautiful she was. "How come you didn't learn to read, Grandmother?"

"Because nobody knew how to read back then, on the farm. You just took care of your animals and everyone traded with each other. There wasn't much use for reading unless you were in the city." She paused for a moment. "There was one book, however, that we knew from beginning to end. That is the book that has guided us all of this time."

"What book was that?" Zeba asked.

Grandma smiled. "The Qur'aan."

Zeba realized sheepishly what a dumb question that had been. She and Wali were memorizing the Qur'aan too, and they were halfway through already. "How did you learn the Qur'aan and what it says if you can't read?"

"Because it was memorized and passed down generation to generation. What I have learned to treasure is the words of Allaah (SWT) telling us how to be the best human beings we can be."

"What does that mean, Grandma?"

Grandma looked away towards the window. A brown-colored wren sat on a branch just outside the window, singing. She contemplated him in silence for a while as she thought about what she wanted to say.

"Allaah (SWT) loves those who have the most moral character," she said finally, turning her attention back to her granddaughter. "That is, people who are always honest, who do the right thing whether someone is there or not, and who are fair to all. These people also hold themselves accountable for everything. Whatever they are given to do, they put in one hundred and ten percent of their effort and do their best, and they do this for the sake of Allaah (SWT). They are wary and wise of all around them, and even choose their friends wisely, because they are aware that the friends they choose will be who they become."

Zeba looked at her grandma. "Those are a lot of good qualities." She thought for a moment. "I think Grandfather and Father are two such people. Am I right?"

Grandma smiled. "Yes, you are correct. When your grandfather first came to ask for my hand, I was careful to ask all around about who he was. I wanted to make sure he was a good man, and everyone I asked spoke highly of him. At one time, I even got a little scared and thought he might be too good for me."

Zeba gave a little laugh. "Really, Grandma, why would you say that? You're beautiful, wise, and so patient. I couldn't even imagine you and Grandpa not being together."

Grandma thanked Zeba for the kind words, and continued, "The reason your Grandpa and I can get along so well is because we both have very high moral standards, and we do everything for the sake of Allaah (SWT). Alhamdulillaah, thanks to those lessons we were taught as children, we were able to avoid many of the problems that exist today."

Zeba was puzzled. "What do you mean by 'problems that exist today'?"

Grandmother looked deep into Zeba's eyes. "There are many problems that exist today, little one, because people have forgotten Allaah (SWT). Too many couples no longer stay together after they are married. Divorce rates are high and seem to go higher still every year. Murder has become so commonplace people hardly even give it a thought anymore unless it touches them directly. People become addicted to drugs, alcohol, and smoking. Depression and other psychological problems have been on the rise in the past few years. People are no longer reading the book of Allaah (SWT) or following its guidance. They mistakenly think they can guide themselves and that they already know the purpose to life. It's sad to see so many people go through what they do, only because they don't know the Secret to Life."

Zeba sat up and moved closer to Grandma. "The Secret? What's that?"

Grandma held Zeba's hand. "The Secret is in knowing why we were sent down to earth and what our purpose in life is. If we know that, then we can solve any problem big or small without giving up. We can face anything that is thrown at us, for we are stronger than steel. Yet we have mercy as well, for we have discovered the truth. We learn to have compassion for others, as well as to serve others. We practice kindness and generosity in our lives, not selfishness and greed, and we live our lives in accordance with the rules and etiquettes that were given to us from Almighty Allaah (SWT). We forgive those who do us evil, for we know that's the way to keep the heart calm and happy. We have tolerance for everyone, for we are all the creatures of Allaah (SWT). You see, Zeba, when we lead by example, we help change this world into a better one. Always remember, whether you set an example for good or for evil, if your example is a strong one, someone will follow it."

Zeba's mother walked by the room and saw them talking together. "Assalaamu-alaykum, may I join in?"

"Why of course," said Grandma.

Zeba made space for her mom to sit next to them. "Mom, Grandma is teaching me about the Secret," she said enthusiastically.

Her mom smiled. "The Secret? Does it have anything to do with Prophet Muhammad (PBUH)?"

Grandma returned her smile. "I was just getting to that." She turned again to Zeba. "The best way for us to learn is through the example of the greatest man who ever lived."

"The Prophet Muhammad (PBUH)," Zeba said.

"Yes," her grandmother said, nodding. "You see, he lived his life following all of those rules, and he is an example for all to learn from. He was a great leader, but because people are not really following the path that he laid out for them, they fall into error and they are unhappy, and their unhappiness expresses itself in many ways. But those who truly follow Islam from its core foundation will know genuine happiness and will live their lives at peace with themselves and all others."

Zeba looked at her mother. "Mom, is that why you counsel all those women? They come to you and you help them solve their problems?"

Her mom looked sadly at her. "Yes. I feel so sorry for those people; they think their problems are so huge, when they are actually quite small. Every problem can be solved very quickly should they have the wisdom to understand that Allaah (SWT) does not give us more than we can handle. Allaah (SWT) does not give us a illness, whether it is of the body or the spirit, without giving us a cure to it as well."

Zeba was amazed. This was the first time her mom had spoken about her counseling. She looked at her mom and wondered how this woman with no education, who had never studied psychology, could help so many with their problems.

Zeba did not realize it consciously, but she was now experiencing what her grandmother called wisdom. Her mother and grandmother were talking, but Zeba had gone deep into her own thoughts.

What if one could have both wisdom and education, she wondered? What a combination that would be. Would you be able to help many more people? More and more questions arose in her mind.

Her grandma and mother got up to go to bed. "Assalaamu-alaykum, Zeba," they both said.

"Wa'alaykum assalaam," Zeba responded.

She was tired as well. She said her du'aas and soon fell fast asleep.

"If you learn from every experience, you are heading for greatness"
Zohra Sarwari

What is character? Character is defined as an attribute or feature that makes up and distinguishes an individual. This could be a good thing or a bad thing. Establishing good character is key to an individual's success. Some of the distinguished characteristics of successful people are wisdom seeking, integrity, honesty, and justice. Character building starts at home, but sometimes people are not exposed to it due to life circumstances, and kids are not taught these topics. Due to not being taught or choosing not to focus on these qualities, kids can stray and take the wrong paths in life.

I want to discuss some of these character builders that are vital to one's success. However, one can develop these qualities anytime they choose to. They are easily learnable.

What is wisdom? Wisdom is when one must logically identify conscious convicting truth to be intellectually honest. People who have high character and high ethics tend to search for something other than knowledge or intelligence, such as searching and finding what is right or true. Wisdom is rarely seen in our youth and adults nowadays. It's a rare quality; therefore, to become extraordinary humans, find wisdom within you on a constant basis. Then and only then will you truly see what success is. Start with the search for God. Who is God, and which religions believe in God? How did the three major religions emerge? What are Islam, Christianity and Judaism? By asking these questions, we can seek the truth. Ignorance leads us astray, while truth leads to wisdom. What are the commonalities between these three religions, and where do they differ? What are the Books of God? They are the 'Qur'aan', the 'Torah', and the 'Gospel of Jesus' (PBUH). Did you know the Qur'aan is the only Book of God that has never changed or been altered. It is in its original form since it was first revealed 1400 years ago. In search for the truth one should read all of these books to better understand the religion that Allaah (SWT), God the Greatest has sent down to us.

What is integrity? Integrity is when an individual does what he or she says he will do. People of integrity usually have great conviction to do what they say they will do, regardless if there is great pressure for them to do otherwise. For example, there was a woman who got shot in the head while walking with her three-year-old daughter to pick up her other children from school. The reason she was shot was because she was wearing a headscarf. This scared many women, and some even took off their headscarf. Many told me it was unsafe to wear my headscarf. Yet it only made me stronger. I am proud of whom I am and I wear the headscarf only to please my Lord. I couldn't understand that we have to come to a day when it is okay to walk down the street with a two-piece bikini, but not covered up. I will not change who I am, for my integrity as a Muslim woman is strong.

What is honesty? Honesty is the quality that humans possess when they are communicating with truth. They can show this not only by speaking, but also by their actions and body language. Honest people tend to take responsibility for their errors and not blame others. High character people tend to watch their tones and break bad habits like cynicism and sarcasm. High character people who are honest also tend to be compassionate. Honesty is an ingredient to the formula of success.

What is justice? Justice is upholding the truth and correcting wrongs. People who are just do not condemn powerless people or oppress people. Instead, they help them and protect them. They just believe in doing the right thing. Humans innately know what is right and what is wrong, regardless of their race, color, and religion. If everyone searched within himself or herself to seek justice, we would not have injustice. Being just is an ingredient to becoming successful.

Why is character building important? When one holds himself up to very high standards, then one often thinks of everything they are doing. From the way they speak to how they act; whether they give to charity in secret or in open. They criticize themselves before others can criticize them. They hold themselves accountable to everything they say or do. They want to lead by example, not by being a hypocrite. It can take deep searching within oneself to find this quality that we all possess. Most importantly, we need to ask our Creator for guidance with this topic. Only then will we know who we really are and our true purpose and passion in life. This is the stage all humans should try to achieve. This will lead them to greatness they never knew existed in them. They will be great at everything they do, and regrets will be a thing of the past. This is one of the levels of achieving excellence. I strongly believe that each and every one of us is able to achieve this greatness. Only when we can achieve it can we teach it.

Respect is important to character building. Respect means to treat people the same way you would want to be treated. When we realize that we are the same, regardless of race, religion or gender, we are much more able to get along with others and treat them with the same dignity with which we would treat a poor person or a rich person. No situation or outside circumstances matter when speaking to someone. If we are able to blend in any situation and be respectful, then we have achieved another part of the formula to success. Respect, like all of the other great qualities, begins within oneself. If we can respect ourselves first, then we can learn to respect our parents, our siblings, our families, our communities, and anyone we are in contact with. Start within yourself first, and then expand out.

What is excellence? Excellence is when we do our best and continue to push ourselves to do better; when we won't settle for less. When we know that every choice we make will define who we want to become. Excellence requires at times doing the right thing, even if it is risky and costly. We achieve excellence when our standards are higher than average. When one achieves excellence, we also become highly competent.

Who are our companions? Companions are those people whom we are closest to. Sometimes they can be family members, but most of the time they will be people who we associate with who are outside our family scope. It is vital for us to know that our companions will make us or break us. If we have the right companions or group of friends, then success shall come to us at a faster rate than when we are alone. However, should we have the wrong companions or friends; we will suffer a great deal. So much sometimes, that we won't even realize it until it's too late.

Did you know that the five people you hang around with the most are that whom you will be most like? Your income will also be the average of those five people. Imagine if you hang around with people who are on welfare. You can end up on welfare. However, if you hang around people who are successful, just by association and being in their presence, your chances for success are very high. Choose whom you spend your time with wisely. For it can make you or break you.

What is compassion? Compassion is an emotion one feels for someone who is suffering. Most people who are compassionate like to help those whom they think are suffering. Showing special kindness to those who suffer is another powerful ingredient to success. Compassion is essential to become a great leader and to be successful. Zig Ziglar's most famous quote is, *"If you help enough people get what they want, you will get what you want."* By being compassionate and helping people solve their problems, we can become successful. Don't help someone because you want something in return; help him or her because you are able to. A great expression we have in Dari (Eastern Persian spoken in Afghanistan) is: *"Always do good, and then throw what you did in a river."* Never look back to expect anything; it's amazing how Allaah (SWT) will give it back to you in ways that you never expected, especially, if you do the good deeds for the sake of Allaah (SWT). As a Muslim, I highly believe in doing good things only for the sake of Allaah (SWT). By doing good deeds for that purpose alone, my standards will always be held up high. Many have asked me, *"How about doing good deeds just because it feels good to do them?"* I answer, *"What will happen if I am not in a good mood? I don't do good deeds?"* By being held responsible for everything we say or do, just keeps me more aware and conscious to always try my best; for I pray that Allaah (SWT) will take care of me and my family in the hereafter.

What is the definition of a leader? A leader is one who has the ability to influence, motivate, and enable others to contribute towards the ultimate goal they are working on. A great leader should possess all the qualities that I have described above plus more. Great leaders are one in a million. Lately, the number of great leaders has decreased and the number of bad leaders has increased. That's why I am discussing it in this book. It is a vital part of the formula to success to know what a great leader is. Great leaders sacrifice themselves for those they lead. They lead by example. Great leaders tend to produce great leaders after them. Everyone is a leader in one sense or another. For example, an eldest child may be a leader in his home, or any child may be the leader in a school project. So everyone is a leader somewhere in his life. People don't think of themselves as leaders, so they aren't the best they can be. They settle for what is expected of them — or less.

Great leaders look to excel in every aspect of their lives. They know they are not perfect, but always look for avenues to get better and excel. They learn knowledge and implement it in their lives. Our greatest leaders in the past have been sent down from Allaah (SWT) as Messengers or Prophets; those who have guided most of mankind until today. From Prophet Adam, being the first man who existed, to Prophet Abraham, Prophet Moses, Prophet Jesus, and Prophet Muhammad (Peace be upon them all). These great men that Allaah (SWT), God the Most Magnificent sent to mankind are the best examples of what leaders should be. I would like to give some examples here of what non-Muslims say about the Prophet Muhammad (PBUH):

"I wanted to know the best of the life of one who holds today an undisputed sway over the hearts of millions of mankind ... I became more than ever convinced that it was not the sword that won a place for Islam in those days in the scheme of life. It was the rigid simplicity, the utter self-effacement of the Prophet, the scrupulous regard for pledges, his intense devotion to his friends and followers, his intrepidity, his fearlessness, his absolute trust in God and in his own mission. These and not the sword carried everything before them and surmounted every obstacle. When I closed the second volume (of the Prophet's biography), I was sorry there was not more for me to read of that great life."

-Mahatma Gandhi, statement published in 'Young India', 1924

"If any religion had the chance of ruling over England, nay Europe, within the next hundred years, it could be Islam.

I have always held the religion of Muhammad in high estimation because of its wonderful vitality. It is the only religion, which appears to me to possess that assimilating capacity to the changing phase of existence, which can make it appeal to every age. I have studied him - the wonderful man, and in my opinion far from being an anti-Christ, he must be called the Savior of Humanity.

I believe that if a man like him were to assume the dictatorship of the modern world he would succeed in solving its problems in a way that would bring it the much needed peace and happiness:
I have prophesied about the faith of Muhammad that it would be acceptable to the Europe of tomorrow as it is beginning to be acceptable to the Europe of today."

-Sir George Bernard Shaw, 'The Genuine Islam', Vol. 1, No. 8, 1936

"My choice of Muhammad to lead the list of the world's most influential persons may surprise some readers and may be questioned by others, but he was the only man in history who was supremely successful on both the secular and religious level ... It is probable that the relative influence of Muhammad on Islam has been larger than the combined influence of Jesus Christ and St. Paul on Christianity ... It is this unparalleled combination of secular and religious influence which I feel entitles Muhammad to be considered the most influential single figure in human history."

-Michael Hart in 'The 100, A Ranking of the Most Influential Persons In History', New York, 1978

"Four years after the death of Justinian, A.D. 569, was born in Mecca, in Arabia, the man who, of all men, has exercised the greatest influence upon the human race ... To be the religious head of many empires, to guide the daily life of one-third of the human race, may perhaps justify the title of a Messenger of God."

-Dr. William Draper in 'History of Intellectual Development of Europe'

"No other religion in history spread so rapidly as Islam. The West has widely believed that this surge of religion was made possible by the sword. But no modern scholar accepts this idea, and the Quran is explicit in the support of the freedom of conscience.

Like almost every major prophet before him, Muhammad fought shy of serving as the transmitter of God's Word sensing his own inadequacy. But the Angel commanded 'Read'. So far as we know, Muhammad was unable to read or write, but he began to dictate those inspired words which would soon revolutionize a large segment of the earth: 'There is one God'.

In all things Muhammad was profoundly practical. When his beloved son Ibrahim died, an eclipse occurred and rumors of God's personal condolence quickly arose. Whereupon Muhammad is said to have announced, 'An eclipse is a phenomenon of nature. It is foolish to attribute such things to the death or birth of a human being'.

At Muhammad's own death an attempt was made to deify him, but the man who was to become his administrative successor killed the hysteria with one of the noblest speeches in religious history: 'If there are any among you who worshiped Muhammad, he is dead. But if it is God you worshiped, He lives forever'."

-James Michener in 'Islam: The Misunderstood Religion', Reader's Digest, May 1955, pp. 68-70

"History makes it clear, however, that the legend of fanatical Muslims sweeping through the world and forcing Islam at the point of sword upon conquered races is one of the most fantastically absurd myths that historians have ever repeated."

-De Lacy O'Leary in 'Islam at the Crossroads', London, 1923

"He was sober and abstemious in his diet and a rigorous observer of fasts. He indulged in no magnificence of apparel, the ostentation of a petty mind; neither was his simplicity in dress affected but a result of real disregard for distinction from so trivial a source.

In his private dealings he was just. He treated friends and strangers, the rich and poor, the powerful and weak, with equity, and was beloved by the common people for the affability with which he received them, and listened to their complaints.

His military triumphs awakened neither pride nor vain glory, as they would have done had they been affected for selfish purposes. In the time of his greatest power he maintained the same simplicity of manners and appearance as in the days of his adversity. So far from affecting a regal state, he was displeased if, on entering a room, any unusual testimonials of respect were shown to him. If he aimed at a universal dominion, it was the dominion of faith; as to the temporal rule which grew up in his hands, as he used it without ostentation, so he took no step to perpetuate it in his family."

-Washington Irving, 'Mahomet and His Successors'

"The lies (Western slander) which well-meaning zeal has heaped round this man (Muhammad) are disgraceful to us only.

A silent great soul, one of that who cannot but be earnest. He was to kindle the world; the world's Maker had ordered so."

-Thomas Carlyle in 'Heroes and Hero Worship and the Heroic in History', 1840

I have included other people's quotes, for I want everyone to be able to read the Biography of the Greatest Man who lived. If one wants to see how a true leader was, then they should read the biographies of all the greatest leaders that existed, starting with the Messengers of Allaah (SWT); Adam, Ibrahim (Abraham), Lut (Lot), Musa (Moses), Eisa (Jesus), and Muhammad (Peace Be Upon Them All).

Greatness

Greatness can mean anything to anyone. For the purpose of my book, I will tell you what greatness means to me. Greatness means to me being the best of who you are regardless of the situation you are in. It doesn't matter if you're poor or rich, short or tall, white or black. It means that despite the circumstances that were thrown at you, you are able to overcome that adversity and succeed.

The most phenomenal example that I can tell you about is the Prophet Muhammad (PBUH). When archangel Jibreel first revealed to the Prophet the message of Islam, he (PBUH) was scared and shaking, for he had never been in a situation as that one. However, the Prophet Muhammad (PBUH) began conveying the message he was given to all of humankind. Imagine a time of idol worship, and horror. It was in this time that the final revelation of the religion of Islam began (1) as a call to all humans to submit to Allaah (SWT), to restore the monotheist faith of Abraham once again, and to bring all people to the same path of righteousness and goodness. You can only imagine the reaction of these people. Idol worship was the basis of their business. People from all over Arabia used to bring money to the Makkans in order to take care of their gods. All of Makkah got annoyed at the Prophet's message and wanted to stop the spread of Islam, for it was going to ruin their business by driving away the contributions of the idol worshipers. It was at this time that the richest Arabs who lived in Makkah offered the Prophet Muhammad (PBUH), through his uncle, everything he could possibly desire. They offered him anything he wanted; money, large homes, wives, and even the status of being the King of Makkah. However, Prophet Muhammad (PBUH) rejected their offerings. Here we had a man that the idol worshipers would give anything to, just to stop preaching that there was only one God. Yet, he did not accept. Even when they tortured Muslims, beat them, persecuted them and exiled them, they still held on to their belief, that there is only one God, and Muhammad was His last and final messenger. His greatness came from who he was as a man, his morals, his values, his impeccable character, his honesty, his patience, etc.

I believe that he is greatest example for all of humankind to look up to, as are all the other Prophets of Allaah (SWT): Adam, Abraham, Noah, Joseph, John the Baptist, Lot, Moses, Jesus (PBUT) and many other Prophets. There are many great examples, and we should read about them to learn who they were and what made them the great examples that they were.

The next example, of greatness will be of one of my favorite Muslim scholars of my lifetime. His name is Dr. Abu Ameenah Bilal Philips. Dr Bilal was born in Jamaica, but grew up in Canada, where he accepted Islam in 1972 after earlier converting from Christianity to communism. He completed a diploma in Arabic and a BA at the Islamic University of Madeenah in 1979, an MA in Islamic Theology at the University of Riyadh, in 1985, and a PhD in Islamic Theology in the department of Islamic Studies at the

---

(1)   Islam began with Prophet Adam, the first human and the first prophet of Islam.

University of Wales in 1994. Abu Ameenah taught Islamic Education and Arabic in private schools in Riyadh for over ten years, lectured M.Ed students in the Islamic Studies department of Shariff Kabunsuan Islamic University in Cotobato City, Mindanao, Philippines, founded and directed the Islamic Information Center in Dubai, United Arab Emirates and the Foreign Literature Department of Dar al Fatah Islamic Press in Sharjah, UAE, lectured in Arabic and Islamic Studies at the American University in Dubai and Ajman University in Ajman, UAE (www. bilalphilips.com), founded and headed the Department of Arabic and Islamic Studies at Preston University, Ajman, UAE, and is currently the Dean of the Islamic Studies Academy in Doha, Qatar (www.islaamicstudiesacademy.com).

His greatness lies in the fact that he was born and raised as a non-Muslim, Christian who became a communist in a quest to find a way of life which would bring justice and equality to the world, only to find the object of his quest in Islam. However, he did not stop there; instead he struggled to educate himself in Islam and went on to become a great scholar, teacher, speaker, and author. There are very few people who have the ability to inspire others, and he is one of them. Listening to him speak makes one want to listen more. You do not want that conversation to end, for it is very deep and impacting *alhamdulillaah*.

The two examples that I have given are to show you that greatness is fundamentally a blessing from Allaah. Sometimes it is a special blessing – not available to others, as in the case of Prophet Muhammad (PBUH), and most often it is a blessing which lies within the reach of each and every one of us; all we need to do is discover it. Money might not be attached to this greatness at all. Instead, there might be inspiration, motivation, and knowledge, or many other things attached to your greatness. Remember that if you love what you do, and do it well, the money might just come along with it. Yet, if there is no money you will still be happy. That is discovering your true gift, and potential.

Forgiveness

How does one learn to love everyone? Learning to love is one of the most powerful things one can do. One can love greatly if one can learn to forgive.

What does it mean to forgive? One with high character has to constantly remember that no person is perfect. They have to constantly ask for forgiveness and seek to forgive others. Forgiveness is among the best feelings ever. I would like everyone to do an exercise here: write a letter and ask everyone you know for forgiveness. The letter should be concise and clear. It should be from your heart. After this letter is written, it should be passed to everyone you know. You will be astonished with what happens afterwards. Not only will you feel great about what you did, but also you will blossom new relationships with old enemies. You might even be able to guide them to make themselves better humans.

I will share with you a letter I wrote about forgiveness:

Assalaamu-alaykum to all of you,

I hope this letter reaches all of you in good health. I would like to start off by saying thank you for opening up this letter. That alone means you're willing to at least see what I have to say. Ahsan jan and I had an experience that was phenomenal. We had some epiphanies from a trip we took recently and discovered what well-being meant to us.

One thing that well-being meant to us was forgiveness; I could not explain that word in more depth if I tried. That word has a different meaning to each of us. For me, it means to have no hard feelings against anyone; to have my heart open to everyone; to unite as a family, as well as friends. To have unconditional love for everyone regardless of where they are in their lives, what they have chosen to do with their lives, and how they seek happiness.

So here goes one of the hardest questions that you will face. Can you find a place in your heart to forgive me? Some of you might mention that I have not done anything to you, but because in life we do not always know whose feelings we have hurt or not, I am addressing this letter to everyone I can. I want you all to know that as a human being I have made my share of mistakes. I have hurt people with words, actions, stories, etc. I can see clearly my mistakes; I do not need to die for Allaah (Subhaanahu wa ta'ala) to show me my mistakes. This is why I feel I have been bothered for some time now. I have always wanted to live a life of happiness and well-being. I have discovered what it means to live that way. It is more than words can explain. I feel that I have changed tremendously already inside. However, it is not good enough for me to feel good inside when none of you feel good about what I have done. It will mean the world to me to start a new life with each other.

When I see each one of you I have a new feeling towards you. I only feel happiness towards you. I only feel love towards you. I want you to know that no matter what happens I will not judge you, nor talk behind your back, nor hate you, nor disguise a relationship with you. I want you to know that if you ever need a friend, sister, or cousin that you can count on me. I want you to know that true happiness is within each one of us.

For the first time in my life I know what real happiness is, and I will try to live it that way for the rest of my life. I will try to enjoy each moment I have with each of you as if it's the last moment we share together. I will love and enjoy my husband, children, family, friends, employees, and anyone else I meet as if they are the best of who they are. However, my enjoyment will not be as fulfilling without your forgiveness. Your forgiveness will mean an eternity to my family and me. I see the past as being gone. The past does not exist. And nobody owns the future. All we have is the here and now, the present. So that is why I want to start anew with all of you. I want to create moments that we will treasure for the rest of out lives. By this time you are all wondering what I am on? LOL!! Nothing, just wisdom and enlightenment from Allaah (Subhaanahu wa ta'ala). We are all so blessed in our own ways, and I am very, very thankful for all that my family and I have been blessed with.

I pray that Allaah brings each of you the happiness and joy that your hearts desire, and that you all be blessed with your families. May you have an infinite amount of joy and excitement with whichever way life's journey takes you.

This letter is addressed to everyone that I know. I apologize if I could not personally e-mail this letter to some of you; it is because I did not have your email addresses. Also this letter is addressed to your parents as well. Please share this letter with all of your relatives I know. I tried my best to find as many of you as I can. So please feel free to forward it.

I thank you from the bottom of my heart for reading this letter, because I know your time is precious.

Sincerely Yours,

Zohra Sarwari

Tolerance

Tolerance is another powerful ingredient in your quest for success. I love discussing tolerance, for it is the most powerful habit to acquire. I would like to start off by giving some examples of people using tolerance to its highest accord. The examples are all of Allaah's (SWT) Prophets, who were sent to the people. It is through their tolerance that so much good has occurred in history. Without them helping us and leading us to the right path, I know we would have been totally lost as a human race. Examples of tolerance from the Prophet Muhammad (PBUH):

One old woman made a habit of throwing rubbish on Prophet Muhammad (PBUH) whenever he passed from her house. Prophet Muhammad (PBUH) had to pass that house daily on the way to the mosque. Even when the old woman threw rubbish on him, he would pass silently without showing any anger or annoyance. This was a regular, daily event.

One day when Prophet Muhammad (PBUH) was passing by the woman was not there to throw the rubbish. Prophet Muhammad (PBUH) stopped and asked the neighbor about her well-being. The neighbor informed the Prophet Muhammad (PBUH) that the woman was sick in bed. The Prophet Muhammad (PBUH) politely asked permission to visit the woman. When allowed he entered the house, the woman thought that he had come there to take his revenge when she was unable to defend herself because of sickness. But the Prophet Muhammad (PBUH) assured her that he had come to her, not to take any revenge, but to see her and to look after her needs, as it was the command of Allaah (SWT) that if anyone is sick, a Muslim should visit and help him if needed.

There are many more such examples which show the Prophet Muhammad's (PBUH) tolerance. Other examples would include Mahatma Gandhi and his tolerance for others regardless of their race, religion, or gender. Had he not been tolerant, he would not have been as successful as he was.

Martin Luther King Jr. is another example. There are many more examples, which is why it is important for us to read biographies of the greatest people who lived. We can learn so much from them.

I am a big believer of tolerance. We all need to make it a habit in our lives. By having tolerance we will be better equipped for the changing world and we can get along much better with one another. Respect will be amongst us all, and our knowledge will increase to help better understand why we do the things we do. Tolerance can be one of the most powerful tools we possess. Very few people have this habit or even attempt to try to learn what tolerance really is.

Exercises

I would like you to do the next few exercises to develop your character into excellence. The first exercise will be to not lie for two weeks. No matter what happens, control yourself and commit to yourself that you will be honest. Make a daily diary and write down when you wanted to fib or tell a small lie but avoided it. You controlled yourself. You will see that after seven days it becomes habit. However, after two weeks, it will be more instilled in you. If you really want to change a habit, do it with full power.

The second exercise I want you to do is be nice regardless of the circumstances. Smile at everyone you come in contact with. Be cheerful. Say "hello" first. Thank others for even the smallest thing they do. Help someone without expecting anything in return. Do one nice deed a day and see how your life transforms. The energy you will get from this experience will be phenomenal. Do this exercise for the next two weeks as well. Force yourself, if you have to. Even a smile is charity. No excuses. Challenge yourself!

The last exercise will require you to put 110% in everything you do. Whether you are working out, eating healthy, working at your job, talking to someone, reading, doing homework, do your BEST! Do more than your BEST. Push yourself to go beyond your limits. That's when your confidence will BLOW up. Take MASSIVE ACTION with these exercises and you will be at another level within two weeks. You won't believe how much you have changed. You are on your way to SUCCESS.

Situations when you controlled yourself and didn't lie:

1--

2--

3--

4--

5--

6--

7--

8--

9--

10 --

Was nice regardless of the circumstance; 14 nice deeds done in 14 days:

Week 1

1--

2--

3--

4--

5--

6--

7--

Week 2

1--

2--

3--

4--

5--

6--

7--

Extra Good Deeds Done!

Step 3:

Working for Profits
and Not Wages

Over the next few days, Zeba pondered at length the wisdom her mother and grandmother had shared with her.

This was what she especially loved about being at home: she received lessons about life that she probably would not receive elsewhere. Even though her parents were not educated, they were very smart and wise, and in spending her days with them and her grandparents, she was exposed to an array of knowledge that made her more mature and wiser than other girls her age. People often thought she was seventeen or eighteen years old instead of just thirteen.

Some of the parents of her friends were very smart as well, but when she asked them questions, she was often surprised by how much they did not know about the important things of life, the sort of things about which her parents and grandparents talked to her often.

Zeba wanted to be well-rounded. She wanted to be book smart, but she also wanted to know how to cook and do other tasks; knowledge that would in time be an important asset to her as a wife and mother. She wanted to learn more than these things, though. She was an honest person, and loved to take care of her family. She respected her parents deeply, and was also very patient. She loved to learn, and wasn't shy in asking how things were done the way they were, or why.

Zeba was reading 'The Greatest Salesman in the World' one afternoon when Wali walked into her room. "Assalaamu-alaykum, Zeba," he greeted her. "Have you figured out what the gold in the book is yet?"

"No, but I found out what the secret to this life is," she said with a happy smile. "I always knew it, but I discovered a different meaning to it the other day. It's amazing. Would you like me to share it with you?"

Wali smiled back at her. "Grandma told you? I thought she would have waited awhile longer, but I guess she thought the timing was right."

Zeba looked confused. "I had no idea that people had so many problems in their lives. I have been so naive. SubhaanAllaah, Allaah (SWT) has been great to us. We should never forget our prayers, and never stop
doing good deeds. Allaah (SWT) loves those who are best in morals and character."

"You're right, we should never stop being thankful to Allaah (SWT). There are so many stories I will share with you when the time is right, to help you better understand life. For now, though, I want to ask you about the book."

Zeba looked happy and said, "I can't wait for those stories, and yes I am ready to talk about the book."

"Let me go get my notes then and we'll discuss some main concepts together, to see if you're able to understand the big picture." Wali was back moments later with his notebook. He surprised her by saying, "Zeba, after I talk to you about this new way to approach life, I want us to start our own business. What do you think?"

Zeba scratched her head. "Start our own business? Do we have the resources to do that?"

"Yes, we do, we just have to work very hard and follow through with the plans, and be patient. Are you interested in working with me on this project?"

Zeba nodded. "Yes. If we could succeed at this, it could help the whole family."

"Bingo, that's exactly what I think," Wali said with a happy grin. "Okay, let's get started."

Zeba got her notepad and pen ready, and nodded that she was ready for him to begin.

"Do you know the difference between profits and wages?" Wali asked.

Zeba looked at him, thought of the book, and replied, "I think so. Isn't wages when you work for someone else, and profits when you work for yourself?"

Wali nodded approvingly. "Yes, that's the essence of it. The big difference, you see, is that when you work for someone else, for wages, you must work and think as they dictate. When you work for yourself, on the other hand, you can be very creative, and creativity is the key to making a great deal of money. What you do with that money, however, is what is most important."

"What should one do with the money he makes, then?"

"Well, when most people get money, they want to hold on to it tightly, or they squander it on themselves. But that is like damming up a river, it stops the flow of the river and the water becomes stagnant. The first thing one should do with money is to give away ten percent right off the top, to Saddaqa (charity). In that way, the abundance of life continues to flow.

"Next, instead of squandering it, you spend as little as you need to on yourself, and put some of the money away for a rainy day, so that you are prepared for any financial troubles that might befall you.

"Lastly, you save the rest for your big investment project, or investment opportunities. Are you getting this so far, Zeba?"

Zeba stared at him while she thought about what he had just told her. Finally, she said, "I will tell you what I understood. I am to work for myself, be creative, because that's what will make me a lot of money, then give away ten percent, spend as little as possible, save some for an emergency situation, and lastly, save all I can for my investment opportunities."

Wali was surprised at how quickly she had grasped the basics he had shared with her. "That's it! What all of this means is, you have to become an entrepreneur, which is anyone who works for his or herself. It is not easy to be an entrepreneur. If you remember, Hafid, in 'The Greatest Salesman', goes through many trials and tribulations before he gets what he seeks, which is also by that time what he deserves. He risks everything in order to achieve success.

"The reason so many people do not become successful in their efforts is because they are afraid to take a chance. They want to stay in their comfort zone, but that won't help them achieve success. It is more likely to hinder them. Business people are leaders. They have to find a way to lead themselves first, and then they can help others walk that path towards success."

Wali paused and said, "Zeba, I want you to start taking some notes here. First, entrepreneurs have a certain mindset that others do not have. They are goal driven, which just means they set goals for themselves and then work very hard to achieve those goals. You know how you and I set ourselves goals for memorizing the Qur'aan, and we give ourselves deadlines, and then we work at them until we have accomplished our goals? That's what we will be doing for our business as well."

"Yes," Zeba said. "When you explain it like that, I see what you mean."

"As I go over all the traits that entrepreneurs possess, I will put it in examples like that for you, so it makes better sense," Wali said, and waited while Zeba wrote in her notebook.

"Second," he went on when she was ready, "entrepreneurs are customer focused. They think of what their customers want and how they can get it to them. If their customers are satisfied, they will buy from the business owner over and over. For example, we know that our customers here want fresh milk daily, so we wake up extra early, and after tahajjud (voluntary prayer at night) prayers, we milk the cows. Then, Dad and Uncle Omar deliver the milk to everyone's doorsteps, before they rise. Many people are so satisfied with us, that they sometimes give us more money than they should, but, even more importantly, they refer other people to buy fresh milk from us. In that way, our business continues to grow."

Wali paused. "Is this making sense to you? Do you have any questions so far?"

Zeba shook her head. "No, I think I understand what you're telling me."

"Good." He nodded his approval, and went on: "Third, entrepreneurs are always trying to learn new skills. The more skills one has acquired, the more creative he will be. This means entrepreneurs are constantly working on getting new skills to become better at what they do and so climb up the ladder of success. An example of this would be when Dad and Uncle Omar got so busy that delivery got harder for them to do on time for everyone. What did they do then?"

"They hired a few more drivers for only two hours of the morning, to help with deliveries."

"Exactly! At the same time, Dad thought out how to better organize the routes, and planned a different way to effectively get to all the customers on time. You see, Dad picked up these skills from other farmers before he even needed to use them.

"This leads us to number four: the entrepreneur is future-oriented. Even though nobody is guaranteed tomorrow, we should have plans in place, in case it arrives. Never plan too far ahead, but enough to make sure you are ready to get to the next step when the time arrives. Dad always thinks about the things that might happen down the road, and he sees the expansion of his company as a role model for other farmers.

"Five, one of the most important ones to me is the entrepreneur is a self-starter, and one who is ready to take action immediately.

"Lastly, we have number six. _Never give up_. Entrepreneurs persist as Hafid did to get what he wanted. A good way to look at that is will we ever stop working hard to enter Paradise?"

Zeba said, "No way, we will do all it takes to become the best Muslims, so Allaah (SWT) loves us and wants us near him."

Wali was impressed with his little sister's thinking. She was right where he had hoped she would be in learning all this. They would be successful with their endeavor, with the help of Almighty Allaah (SWT).

"Okay we'll stop there for now," he said. "So, I want to know your thoughts on the things I've told you."

Zeba was impressed with her older brother's wisdom. It occurred to her that he took a lot after Dad and Grandpa. "This is very fascinating," she said. "I love how you put everything into steps. It makes it a lot easier to understand. I guess what I most want to know, though, is what we will be doing? I think you and I have these qualities to be entrepreneurs — but what exactly will our business be?"

"Wali, Zeba, its time for afternoon prayer!" their mother called.

Wali looked at Zeba and they looked at the clock and were amazed at how fast the time had gone by. They rushed to make their ablutions and get ready for prayer. They both loved prayer time. Five times a day, the family stood together, and connected with Allaah (SWT). There was so much to be thankful for, and so much to ask for forgiveness, from the One and Only Lord of the universe. It was the most peaceful part of their day, especially when prayer was over and they raised their hands to ask Allaah (SWT) for whatever they needed.

Today Wali and Zeba raised their hands and asked Allaah (SWT) to help them with this new venture they were planning. If it was something that would bring them goodness in this world and the hereafter, they wanted to pursue it; however, should it bring them pain or misery, to themselves or others, then they both wanted Allaah (SWT) to reject it, and not let the plan follow through. As Muslims, they had been taught early on that many times one wanted this or that or the other, but if Allaah (SWT) knew that what was asked for was not good for the individual, then it usually did not happen. They knew that Allaah (SWT) has infinite wisdom, where people only think they know what is best. Regardless of whatever came their way, they always said "Alhamdulillaah" (All Praise is to the One and Only Lord of the universe, Allaah (SWT).

After prayers they had lunch, and finished their chores. They also studied some English, math, history, and science on their own. Since they both loved reading, teaching themselves wasn't very difficult. If Zeba had a question about something she didn't understand, she usually asked Wali, and if he didn't know they would call Nancy, their teacher who lived next door. She was very knowledgeable, and would explain things thoroughly to them.

They prayed again for Maghrib prayer, and finally they had some free time to take up their discussion again before dinner. Wali told Zeba to meet him in his room, and bring her notepad and pen with her.

Their parents loved to see their children get along so well. They hoped that both of their children had great marriages in the future, but they hoped as well that they would continue to be close to each other.

"I'm ready for the answer to this brilliant plan that you have put together," Zeba said when she walked into Wali's well-organized room. "What will be our business?"

Wali was still looking at his notes and organizing his thoughts. "Just a moment," he said. While she waited Zeba began reviewing her notes as well.

After a few minutes, Wali looked up. "The big plan is to come up with several great ideas that will help people solve their problems in daily life," he said. "We need to become inventors; we need to make something that will ease the burden of people's lives."

Zeba loved the idea of becoming an inventor. "I'm all for that," she said. "But, what will we invent, and how does it all work?"

"We'll have to think of something," Wali said. "Let's start meeting regularly to talk more about this. For the present, let's each of us write down ten new goals that we want to achieve. Tomorrow, I'm busy with Dad, and I know you have to help Grandma with some sewing, so we will meet up on Friday after Jummu'ah prayer and compare notes."

Zeba agreed and went to her own room, already excited, to think about her goals. Wali was excited too, thinking about his own thoughts and ideas for this new venture!

They could both hardly wait for their next meeting.

"Working for yourself will always be worth more to you than working for others."
Zohra Sarwari

What is the difference between profits and wages? When one works for someone else in exchange for their work, they are compensated with wages. Nowadays wages are paid in money format. When one gets a job, their wages are usually set at a rate depending on their education and experience. If one works for wages and doesn't have alternate ways to excel them, they can be very poor at the time of retirement. Wages are what we're taught to get. Go to school and get a job. Then you begin to enjoy life. For a few people that might work and those are the people who specialize in one form of education or another. However, for the remaining 95% of the world, that will not be the best way.

Profit is the amount left after expenses, for one who works for himself. One whom works for themselves is called an entrepreneur. Most often entrepreneurs work for themselves to make more money than when working for others. However they have to be ready for the ups and downs in business, and have other income to support them until their business is stable enough to make profits. Once you are able to make more money, you can save your money until you have enough to pay off a home or buy another business. At that time, you can hire people to run your businesses, or rent your other paid-off property, and you start earning profits.

When someone profits from something, they have earned extra income without doing anything. That means all the people who have two or three homes, and their homes sell for a higher price within ten years after they have purchased it, they made profits. Primarily, they didn't do very much for the homes, for they had property management take care of them. However, those properties were working for them. That's what investments do for a person. They become profits. In America, it is very easy to get out of wages and get into profits. One just has to want to do it bad enough. We will discuss the many ways one can earn profits next.

Who is Jim Rohn? Jim Rohn has been internationally honored as one of the most influential thinkers of our time. His profound business philosophy, visionary insight, and motivational messages have made him a popular speaker, writer, and counselor. Over the past 37 years, he has addressed over 5,000 audiences and 3 million people worldwide. He was a poor farm boy from Idaho who became a millionaire by the age of 31. One of the philosophies in life that made him very rich and successful was, *"Profits are better than Wages."* When he figured that out, he implemented it in his life, and his life took off at that point. He earned profits through network marketing. He did that part-time, and worked his day job full-time, until he no longer had to work his day job.

Who is Robert Kiyosaki? **Robert Toru Kiyosaki** is another author, speaker, businessman, and motivational speaker. He has written 18 books thus far, and sold more than 26 million copies combined. His view on the information and industrial age is very fascinating. His teachings on making money work for you; instead of you working for money is phenomenal. He also believes in profits versus wages. He is famous for his 4 quadrants: Employee/Self-Employed versus Business Owner/Investor. Ninety-five percent of the world falls under the first two quadrants; that is Employee/Self-Employed, whereas 5% of the world falls under the quadrant of Business Owner/Investor. When one is a Business Owner and Investor, one is basically retired. This is where we all dream to be, but very few people take the actual actions to achieve it. Robert Kiyosaki also tells you to become an entrepreneur, and one who has others working for him, at the same time learn to invest your money so that it can work for you.

What does it mean to be an entrepreneur? An **entrepreneur** is a person who undertakes and operates a new enterprise or venture and assumes accountability and the risks along with it. On another note, they will take all the reward that comes with the success of the venture or enterprise. An entrepreneur is one who works for him or herself. An entrepreneur is very important to the economy. These are the people who have the skill and initiative to take new ideas, inventions, or services to the market, and make the right choices to make the idea profitable. Entrepreneurs are willing to risk their time, education and life to become the new leaders of tomorrow. Ninety-five percent of new businesses that open fail their first year. So an entrepreneur needs to realize that there is a chance of his failing, and that's okay; without failure there is no success.

Success is when the project, service or idea that the entrepreneur worked on made it through, and their goals were achieved. Once one has tasted success, they always want more. It's the most powerful feeling.

Entrepreneurs are also leaders, they have the ability to influence, motivate, and get others to help contribute to doing good.

What type of traits do entrepreneurs possess? The six most common traits that they all possess are selflessness, decisiveness, energy, commitment, loyalty and integrity. They also have emotional stability, enthusiasm, conscientiousness, tough-mindedness, self-assurance, compulsiveness, and dominance. All of these traits help make them better leaders and business people to deal with. They are self-starters, and take action immediately. Entrepreneurs are also goal driven, customer-focused, team-oriented, skills-oriented, future-oriented, and socially responsible. I will be sharing some stories of people who are entrepreneurs and they possess these skills. Most of these skills are learnable. Don't worry, if you don't think you possess all of these skills you can learn to possess them with the right mentorship and guidance.

How can one become an entrepreneur? Search within yourself and find your passion. Once you have located your passion, put it in an idea format. Get your idea and think what you can do with it that's different from everyone else selling that product. For example, I have someone who loves to knit. I told her to put a knit kit together and sell it along with a book teaching how to knit. At this point, you're probably thinking "Okay, so what next?" Next we have to learn how to market what you want to sell. Who will be most likely to buy it? Find a market for your product. We will discuss business plans later in the book, and I suggest making a business plan and then moving to the next step.

In the beginning, expect the unexpected. People might be very negative towards what you are doing. You might not have enough funds. You might constantly think you're failing. This is when you need to read this step of the book over and over. You will find stories near the end of this step which will inspire you beyond everything. Those stories will help you climb through your hard times, and help you achieve success.

Most importantly, you have to love what you do. Once you have a passion and a mission, then nothing will stop you from getting to the top. One of my missions is to build orphanages all over the world. I want these orphanage homes to have the best teachers and lots of love. I want to help those kids get educated and make a difference in their countries. My mission is so strong, that I will do everything in my power, and ask Allaah (SWT) to help me achieve my dreams for the sake of doing good for Allaah (SWT). Not only will I hope to be rewarded in this life with the great feelings one gets for helping others and becoming a mentor, but most importantly I pray to be rewarded in the hereafter and that Allaah (SWT) accepts my good deeds. That's what drives me; the hereafter. I try to be the best I can be, for I believe in the hereafter, and I want to do whatever it takes to have a chance for Paradise. No one is guaranteed Paradise, but we all have the same chances to become the best we can be, and to do the things that Allaah (SWT) wants us to do.

Controlling yourself is one of the hardest things to do, but it has the most reward in this life and the hereafter. It shows how strong you really are. Remember that your mission has to be very strong, and then and only then will you succeed. Even if you fail a million times, you will continue trying until you succeed.

Stories of Successful Entrepreneurs

I would like to tell you some more about Oprah Winfrey. She is one of my favorite entrepreneurs, and her story is very inspiring. Being born into a poor family in 1953, she was taught how to read by her grandmother at the age of three. She was hit when she didn't behave or do her chores. She was molested by several family members and a family friend starting at the age of nine. At fourteen, she rebelled, ran away from home and got pregnant, but lost the baby shortly after (www.wikipedia.com). Regardless of this difficult start in her life, in 1971 she was hired by Nashville Air to read the news on air, the same year she enrolled at Tennessee State University. In 1973, she became the first African-American TV correspondent, and the youngest person to co-anchor the news for WTVF-TV. In 1976 she moved to Baltimore to co-anchor the six o'clock news. In 1978 she began a local talk show as co-host. In 1984 she relocated to Chicago to host the morning talk show, called AM Chicago, which became the number one talk show a month later. AM Chicago was renamed Oprah Winfrey in 1985. In 1986, Oprah won a Golden Globe and an Academy Award.

The list goes on and on with all of her accomplishments and the great tributes that she has done, and she's not stopping now. She has achieved greatness regardless of her circumstances. At the age of 32 she was a millionaire. Did she think she would be here today as she is, the richest self-made woman in the world? Her net worth is over $1.5 billion. I wanted to show you that she started with one small thing, and kept her momentum going and look how far she's come. If she can do it, anyone can.

The next story is about the richest man in America, Bill Gates. His story is somewhat different. He was raised with much more prominence; his family was wealthy. His father was an attorney, and his mother was on the board of directors for First Intestate Bank. He attended the best of schools, and was in an environment where his creativity was nurtured. A gift all of us can give to our children if we play our cards right. We can give them environments such as Bill Gates was exposed to, and help them flourish into great achievers. However, environment isn't everything, we still need to be driven and love what we do. Bill Gates had a passion for computers, and he continues making it happen. I would definitely recommend reading about his life as well.

The second richest woman in the world is JK Rowling. JK Rowling grew up in a middle-class home. However, she had seen her share of problems. She got married in 1992, and by December of 1993 she was divorced with a baby. She was also unemployed and living on State benefits. Whenever her daughter Jessica went to sleep, she'd go into different cafes and write. That is when she completed her first book "Harry Potter." She was rejected over and over, until finally someone liked her work. Since then it has all been uphill for her. However, it wasn't an easy trip. It just shows to you that it doesn't matter who you are, what your background is, if you persist in your dreams, eventually the door of success will open.

The next story I will share with you is priceless. Farrah Gray is a kid who made a million dollars at the age of fourteen. He's the youngest African-American to make a million dollars. Farrah's story is unique, for his circumstances were not the norm. He grew up in a single-family home in the ghetto and was the youngest of five kids. He grew up in a home with a lot of love, discipline and spirituality. Faith was an important part of his family life. With love and support from his family, he was nurtured into a great kid. If you get a chance I would advise you to read the book Reallionaire by Farrah Gray. The most important lesson I learned from his book is that it's never too early to start being successful. It doesn't matter what your circumstances are, you can overcome anything. This book opened my eyes and helped me to start my own project.

Read biographies of people who were successful. Just see what they all have in common and how they made it.

Exercises

Write down five biographies that you will read:

1--

2--

3--

4--

5--

Step 4:

Failing Your Way to Success

Zeba sat with her grandmother the following day, sewing clothes for the family. Her grandmother was a great seamstress and was teaching Zeba the ins and outs of sewing. This was Zeba's first lesson and Zeba kept making mistakes. For the first time in her life, she was not good at something she started doing. This frustrated her. She was used to being good at everything she did.

Her grandmother saw the unhappy expression on Zeba's face and paused in her own sewing. "Zeba, no one is naturally talented in everything that they do," she said, sharing a lesson she had lived by for more than sixty years. "Some people are good at one thing and others at another."

"But I want to learn to sew," Zeba said, her expression stubborn.

"As you should, and you can. It is just that, the things you are not good at, you will have to practice over and over, so that eventually you can be good at them."

Zeba smiled. She loved hearing her grandmother's wise words. It always comforted her. No matter how bad the situation or how hard something was, her grandma always made it seem easy. That was what Zeba called wisdom. Zeba realized that she shouldn't get frustrated and upset if something wasn't easy for her to catch on to.

"Zeba, I want to share with you a story about myself, and how I overcame one of the hardest situations in my life. Would you like to hear it?" Grandma asked.

Zeba loved to hear stories, especially true ones. "Oh yes, Grandma, I would be honored if you could share it with me."

Grandmother thought for a moment, then began, "Long ago, when I was about seven years old, my mother was teaching me to memorize the Qur'aan. I did not know how to read, remember, and I was having a hard time with the way the Arabic language was pronounced, so I practiced and practiced, but I wasn't as good as my brothers and sisters. They tried helping me, but I just wasn't getting it. One evening I told my mother that I wasn't going to do it anymore, it was just too difficult for me. My mother asked me to sit on her lap while she told me her story. I was crying by then, I was so upset. My mother wiped the tears from my eyes, and as she did so, I saw that she had tears in her own eyes as well.

"Your great grandmother then told me, 'If you give up now, at this, you will give up all your life, every time something difficult comes your way. But if you continue trying harder and harder, and overcome your obstacle, you will then be able to overcome any obstacle that is thrown at you. I know this seems difficult, but after a little while it will become as easy as one-two-three. Will you just try a little while longer, and see if what I say isn't so?'

"I nodded and thanked my mother for her wisdom, and went back to my lessons. I put in more effort than before, and in a little while, I realized that it wasn't so bad after all. Within about a month after I had actually decided to give up, I was starting to memorize some of the smaller surahs, and a year after that, I was teaching my younger brother how to memorize the surahs. You see, Zeba, had I not failed at learning to memorize the Qur'aan, I might not have learned one of the most important lessons of my life. Through that experience of failing, I learned that if I could memorize something I thought to be extremely difficult, then I was able to do anything.

"I never gave up on anything after that. Every time I wanted to, I remembered my first difficult experience, and how I overcame it. I want to tell you that failure is an important part of one's life. If you do not fail, then how can you succeed? When one fails, they learn to be patient, and find a different way to approach the same problem. That gives you insight and wisdom. Always look at failure as an opportunity to learn more skills and become wise. Is all of this making sense to you, Zeba?"

"Yes, Grandma, this is making a lot of sense." She gave her grandmother a big hug. "You always give me such good advice. Jazaakillaahu khayran, I hope that one day I can do as much for you, as you are doing for me."

Zeba had never before thought of failure as an opportunity. This was advice that she knew she would pass on to her children one day. She made up her mind there and then that she wasn't going to give up, on sewing or anything else. Whatever it was that came up in her life, she was going to keep trying until she figured out how to do it. How wise her grandmother was!

"People will be what they think they are."
Zohra Sarwari

What is the definition of failure? Failure is when one does not achieve his desirable objective. In school, when someone doesn't pass a class, they have failed. **Everyone's definition of failure is somewhat different.** However, most people will agree that failure is when one has set goals and has not achieved them for whatever reason.

There are different types of failure. People can fail in trying to lose weight, pass school, get a job, quitting a bad habit, etc.

Failure means different things to different people. Different folks have different strokes. Failure means one thing to me and another thing to Bill Gates. **We all define it somewhat differently.** However, we all agree that there are three types of people who occupy the world:

1. People who make things happen.
2. People who watch things happen.
3. People who wonder what happened.

I know people who fit in all of these categories. Unfortunately, 50% of the world is people who are wondering what happened. They have no clue what is going on and how it even happened. 45% percent of the world is watching things happen, and 5% of the world is making things happen. Sadly to say, the numbers aren't in our best interest. Which category do you belong in? I have belonged in all three categories at one time or another. It's amazing that most people know of the existence of these three categories, and yet they choose not to change. A lot of people fail once or twice, and do not have the guts to continue trying. They would rather others take their dreams and make them a reality. It's sad but often true.

Failure for adults is much different than failure for children. Children continue trying if they fail, if the correct encouragement is given to them. Adults condition themselves not to overcome their failures. It's easier for them to give up and take the easier route. This is where most kids learn it from.

Failure is very important to success. Without failure one cannot succeed. Without failure one cannot learn.

Failure is essential to learning. Failure is the stepping stone to success. The way I learn best in school is not by being tested, but by discussing the material I wrote about. Don't get me wrong I don't mind tests, but there's just a lot of anxiety that comes with it. I refuse to be under pressure to learn. In college, I learned so much in one class, but didn't pass the tests with flying colors. I was upset for several months. Now when I look back, I realize how dumb that was of me. Although my GPA was always high in college, I feel it was how much I memorized, but not truly learned. I want to go to school, and I love learning, but a test score should not indicate how much I learned. It can make one lose self-confidence. That is why I am home schooling my children. The way some school systems are set up is degrading for many, and the love of learning can be lost in that system. One does not fail in school, if he or she cannot learn the way the system is set up. They just have a different learning style to succeed.

There's a 50% chance of succeeding and 50% chance of failing with every opportunity that one comes across. It's up to the individual to choose whether the glass is half full or half empty. Success is in the eye of the beholder. If they perceive they will succeed, they will. If they perceive they will fail, then they will. They feed themselves what their destiny will be. I always look at every opportunity as a successful one. For I learn from my failures and that is a success on its own.

Murphy's Law is a popular <u>adage</u> in <u>Western culture</u>. It broadly states that things will go wrong in any given situation, if you give them a chance. *"If there's more than one possible outcome of a job or task, and one of those outcomes will result in disaster or an undesirable consequence, then somebody will do it that way"* (www.wikipedia.org). It's usually said; that whatever can go wrong will go wrong. Murphy's Law is very negative. Negativity usually doesn't help one succeed. It's the wrong mental attitude to have. Negativity tends to lead to failure. Sod's Law pretty much say's the same thing. Anything that can go wrong usually will.

I had a friend who always thought negatively. Everything was depressing in her life. Nothing seemed to be going the right way. No matter what happened, she always complained. Sometimes she would be thankful, but 90% of the time, she was negative. I was very sad for her. I felt that if she could change her attitude to great thinking, then she could become great. Her thinking process stopped her from doing a lot of great things in her life.

Positivity is the opposite of negativity; where one is always looking at the glass as half full. I have a great story to share regarding being positive:

> *'John is the kind of guy you love to hate. He is always in a good mood and always has something positive to say. When I would ask him how he was, he replied, "If I were any better, I would be twins!" He was a natural motivator.*
>
> *If an employee was having a bad day, John was there telling the employee how to look on the positive side of the situation. Seeing this style really made me curious, so one day I went up and asked him, "I don't get it! You can't be a positive person all of the time. How do you do it?" He replied, "Each morning I wake up and say to myself, you have two choices today. You can choose to be in a good mood or you can choose to be in a bad mood.*
>
> *"I choose to be in a good mood. Each time something bad happens, I can choose to be a victim or I can choose to learn from it. I choose to learn from it. Every time someone comes to me complaining, I can choose to accept their*

complaining or I can point out the positive side of life. I choose the positive side of life."

"Yeah, right, it's not that easy," I protested.

"Yes, it is," he said. "Life is all about choices. When you cut away all the junk, every situation is a choice. You choose how you react to situations. You choose how people affect your mood. You choose to be in a good mood or bad mood. The bottom line: It's your choice how you live your life."

I reflected on what he said. Soon thereafter, I left the Tower Industry to start my own business. We lost touch, but I often thought about him when I made a choice about life instead of reacting to it.

Several years later, I heard that he was involved in a serious accident, falling some 60 feet from a communications tower. After 18 hours of surgery and weeks of intensive care, he was released from the hospital with rods placed in his back.

I saw him about six months after the accident. When I asked him how he was, he replied, "If I were any better, I'd be twins. Wanna see my scars?"

I declined to see his wounds, but I did ask him what had gone through his mind as the accident took place.

"The first thing that went through my mind was the well-being of my soon-to-be born daughter," he replied. "Then, as I lay on the ground, I remembered that I had two choices: I could choose to live or I could choose to die. I chose to live."

"Weren't you scared? Did you lose consciousness?" I asked.

He continued, "The paramedics were great. They kept telling me I was going to be fine. But when they wheeled me into the ER and I saw the expressions on the faces of the doctors and nurses, I got really scared. In their eyes, I read 'he's a dead man.' I knew I needed to take action."

"What did you do?" I asked.

"Well, there was a big burly nurse shouting questions at me," John said. "She asked if I was allergic to anything. 'Yes, I replied.' The doctors and nurses stopped working as they waited for my reply. I took a deep breath and yelled, 'Gravity!'"

Over their laughter, I told them, "I am choosing to live. Operate on me as if I am alive, not dead."

He lived, thanks to the skill of his doctors, but also because of his amazing attitude ... I learned from him that every day we have the choice to live life fully. Attitude, after all, is everything.

Therefore do not worry about tomorrow, for tomorrow will worry about itself. Each day has enough troubles of its own.'

-Unknown

Stories of People Who Failed Their Way to the Top

1 Andrew Carnegie was born November 25, 1835 in an impoverished household. Although education and money was not in his family, he grew up in a cultured and political home. He was a hard worker, had perseverance, and was always alert to what was happening. It was these qualities of his that brought him many great opportunities. His first job was as a bobbin boy at a cotton mill for $1.20 a week, in the year of 1848. *"By the time he died, Carnegie had given away $350,695,653 (approximately $4.3 billion, adjusted to 2005 figures). At his death, the last $30,000,000 was likewise given away to foundations, charities, and to pensioners"* (www.wikipedia.org).

He is known in history as the Bill Gates of his times, one of the richest men who lived in that era. He started out with poverty, and became a self-made millionaire when all odds were against him. He was not only rich, but a great philanthropist as well.

2 Portrait of an Achiever

- 1832 Failed in Business-Bankruptcy
- 1832 Defeated for legislature
- 1834 Failed in Business-Bankruptcy
- 1835 Fiancée died
- 1836 Nervous Breakdown
- 1838 Defeated in Election
- 1843 Defeated for U.S. Congress
- 1848 Defeated for U.S. Congress
- 1855 Defeated for U.S. Congress
- 1856 Defeated for Vice President
- 1858 Defeated for U.S. Senate

Had you stopped there, you would have missed the final point:

- **1860 Elected President of the United States of America: Abraham Lincoln.**

"His formal education consisted of about 18 months of schooling from unofficial teachers. In effect he was self-educated, studying every book he could borrow. He once walked 20 miles just to borrow one book. His favorite book was, "The Life of George Washington." He mastered the Bible, William Shakespeare's works, English history and American history, and developed a plain writing style that puzzled audiences more used to grandiloquent rhetoric. He was a local wrestler and skilled with an axe; some rails he

had allegedly split in his youth were exhibited at the 1860 Republican National Convention, as the party celebrated the poor-boy-made-good theme. He avoided hunting and fishing because he did not like killing animals even for food and, though unusually tall and strong, spent so much time reading that some neighbors suspected he must be doing it to avoid strenuous manual labor" (www.wikipedia.org).

Here we have a man who was positive, regardless of what the situation was. Although it would seem that he would never succeed, he became the president of the United States of America. He had a great attitude, and was persistent all the way until the end. Attitude + Persistence = Success. Think about the importance that a positive attitude has on every person. You might not see the effect of your attitude today or tomorrow, but eventually you will see the results.

Abraham Lincoln said, *"Give me six hours to chop down a tree, and I will spend the first four hours sharpening the axe."* Basically, he would spend the first four hours working on himself, changing and bettering who he is, and the last two hours on the actual task.

The average person would grab the axe, dull or not, and start chopping away at the tree. Once they realize they're getting nowhere with the tree, they'll give up. However, if they knew that how they held the axe and how they swung it were all different strategies that can help them cut the tree, would they be different? If they knew that the axe needs to sharpen itself in every way possible, so that it can be successful, would their approach to cutting down the tree be different?

You are the axe; you need to constantly be working on bettering yourself in order to survive all the different situations that you face in your life. That could be gaining weight, and knowing how to lose it. That could be learning a different language, and using it while visiting somewhere. Most importantly that could be belief in Allaah (SWT), God the Greatest. That no matter what happens in life, it happens for a reason, and you should always do your best to understand, and learn from it. To continue learning not only helps you but helps society as a whole.

3 The next individual I will discuss is Thomas Edison. Thomas Edison went to school for about three months at the age of seven. He asked too many questions and frustrated the teacher. His mother found out what the teacher thought of him, and decided she would home school him instead. She instinctually knew her son had qualities of intelligence. When Thomas was about eleven years old, his parents taught him how to use the library resources. He began reading as many books as he could at that time. It was then that his parents taught him to be selective in his reading. It was this skill that led him to prefer learning on his own.

By the age of twelve, Tom had already talked his parents into letting him sell candy and newspapers on the local railroad. This led him to selling fruits and vegetables, and at the age of fourteen he exploited his access to the associated news releases that were teletyped into the station each day and published them in his own little newspaper.

"Thomas Edison tested over 3000 filaments before he came up with his version of a practical light bulb" (www.thomasedison.com/brockton.htm).

In his lifetime he had invented 1093 items, and was awarded 1,368 separate and distinct patents.

"Genius is one percent inspiration, ninety-nine percent perspiration."
-Thomas Alva Edison.

If he was a negative thinker, do you think he could get this far?

Failure List of the Famous:

• Einstein was 4 years old before he could speak.

• Isaac Newton did poorly in grade school and was considered "unpromising."

• When Thomas Edison was a youngster, his teacher told him he was too stupid to learn anything. He was counseled to go into a field where he might succeed by virtue of his pleasant personality.

• F.W. Woolworth got a job in a dry goods store when he was 21, but his boss would not permit him to wait on customers because he *"didn't have enough sense to close a sale."*

• Michael Jordan was cut from his high school basketball team.

• Bob Cousy suffered the same fate, but he too is a Hall of Famer.

• A newspaper editor fired Walt Disney because he *"lacked imagination and had no original ideas."*

• Winston Churchill failed the 6th grade and had to repeat it because he did not complete the tests that were required for promotion.

• Babe Ruth struck out 1,300 times, a major league record.

"A person may make mistakes, but is not a failure until he or she starts blaming someone else. We must believe in ourselves, and somewhere along the road of life we will meet someone who sees greatness in us and lets us know it."

-Unknown

Exercises

I want everybody to do a few exercises in the next few minutes to discuss some of their failures. I want to know what you learned from each failure that occurred. Behind every failure is a lesson towards success.

Write down three failures that you have been through, and the results of those failures. Also, what could you have done to turn those failures into success at that time?

1--

2--

3--

Step 5:

Envision Your Dream

Friday was here. Wali and Zeba were both excited to get back to their project, but first they had to get ready to go to Friday prayer. Friday is a special worship day for Muslims; the day when they assembled at the mosque and worshiped Allaah (SWT) together. The whole family loved listening to the lectures and praying with the community. It was a joyous moment for all. After Friday prayer, they greeted their friends and family, and talked for a few minutes. It was the best part of their week and all of them loved Fridays, but today, thinking about their upcoming meeting, Wali and Zeba were even more excited than usual.

When luncheon was over and the dishes washed, Wali and Zeba raced to get their notes and discuss their new project. Wali was sitting at his desk when Zeba joined him in his room, literally hopping up and down with excitement.

"I'm ready, and I have so much to share with you," she declared.

Wali grinned up at her and said, "Me too. Let's get started right away. Tell me, what are the ten dreams or goals that you've set up for yourself?"

Zeba looked down at her paper. "I had so many goals," she said, "but I will just tell you the ten most important ones that I want to accomplish. One, I want to go to Hajj. Two, I want to make it possible for our parents to retire. Three, to take care of Grandma and Grandpa in their old age. Four, I wish to become a scholar of Islam and of business. Five, I would like to have a business that makes me money without my working in it. Six, exercise five times a week. Seven, build mosques in every city. Eight, to establish shelter homes for homeless people. Nine, help women and children get educated. And, ten, I want to get married, and be a great mother."

Wali was smiling by this time. What wonderful goals his younger sister had set for herself. He knew they owed a lot of their thinking and visions to the Qur'aan and the types of books they read, and to their parents as well.

"Zeba, those are wonderful dreams and goals and I'm very proud of you. I know that some of those goals took some effort, and you had to dig deep within yourself to come up with them. Am I correct?"

"Yes, I had to think long and hard about them, and I came up with so many that I decided just to write them all down, and then I chose the ones I thought were most important for today's meeting."

Wali nodded in agreement, and said, "I have many small goals that I have written down as well, that I can work on daily, but I too had to dig deep within me to find the goals that I really wanted to achieve. Insha'Allaah. Here goes my list: my number one goal is the same as yours, to go to Hajj with the family. Second, I want go to Yale University to get the finest education I can get. Third, I too want to retire our parents. Fourth, I want to open a bank that does not use interest in any way. Fifth, I want to become an inventor. Sixth, to have an inventing company, a business that is entirely devoted to thinking up new inventions and making them a reality. Seventh, I would like to open businesses in third world countries and help people there get jobs so they can better their lives. Eighth, I wish to learn the six languages that are used the most in the world. Ninth, to get married to a righteous woman, and raise good, ethical and pious children, and ten, to make my intention in everything I do for the sake of Allaah (SWT), to make sure that all my goals are aligned with what Allaah (SWT) expects from me, and to not do any harm in the way of Islam."

Zeba was listening very carefully. She loved all of her brother's goals. She knew that whatever he put his mind to, he would achieve. He was always proving himself and following through with whatever he said he would do.

"Zeba, how do you feel now that you have said your goals out loud?" Wali asked. "Do you feel stronger about making these goals a reality, because they're not in your head anymore, they're on paper?"

Zeba looked over her paper. "Yes, now that I've told you about them, I feel I must achieve them. Also it has given me more of a vision, now that it is spoken about and written down."

Just then, the adhaan went off. Both Wali and Zeba became silent and waited for the adhaan to end. They made their du'aa and decided they would meet up after prayer to discuss what should be done for the next meeting.

They felt more energized after they had prayed and connected with Allaah (SWT). When they met again in his room, Wali said, "Now that we have talked about our dreams and goals, the next step, as I see it, is for both of us to come up with at least three ideas for a business. The idea has to be something that the two of us can do, without many resources. We have to use our minds and creativity to come up with something that no one else has come up with yet. Are you following me?"

Zeba looked worried, but was up for the challenge. "I'm sure I could come up with a few ideas."

Wali smiled. "Great! I have a few things in my head as well. Let's meet up next week with our lists, and then we can discuss how our ideas might be accomplished."

Zeba went back to her own room. She decided she would begin by going back and looking through some of her books, to see how people in the past had been able to turn thoughts into reality. There were surely many ways in which this could be done, and she needed to search and find them.

She felt that their parents would be so proud when they discovered what she and Wali were up to. For now, though, they would continue to work on it together, just the two of them. In time, when their ideas were further developed, they would share them their parents and grandparents, to get their thoughts and advice.

After a while, Zeba laid her books down and went to work on her chores. Wali continued looking at his notes for a bit longer and wrote some more things down. Then it was time to help his father with the end-of-the-day workload.

Both he and Zeba had the feeling that something great could be happening to them. They were very grateful to Allaah (SWT) for all that they had, especially that He had granted them minds and the intelligence to think with them.

"To Dream Is To Be Alive."
Zohra Sarwari

What does it mean to dream? To dream is to see something others usually don't see. We are all creatures of Allaah (SWT) the Almighty God, and as humans we have a lot in common. Where we're different is that only 5% of us use our gifts to their fullest potential. I have noticed that many people don't dream anymore. Most adults gave up dreaming when they were kids for whatever reason. I am here to tell you guys to never stop dreaming. Those who don't dream can no longer see. To stop dreaming is to end opportunities. To dream is to believe. People who dream are apt to see what they're dreaming. Next is to act on it. For children all of this is different. They can dream big, and imagine it.

How can one dream, and continue that process? Start by setting goals. Goal setting has to be a top priority. Goals are dreams with deadlines. If we don't set any goals how can we accomplish them? Look at small goals as adding up to one large goal in the end. We each have different goals and dreams, but if you take a little bit of action every day, you can achieve extraordinary results. Don't look at a goal as one hard task to accomplish, look at it as small daily tasks to do, and eventually it will give you the results you're looking to get.

It doesn't matter what your goals are, just make them, and start taking massive action to get results for them. So many of us can dream and even write goals down, but never take action to achieve them. Successful people do what unsuccessful people will not do — take action.

No more procrastinating. Too much procrastination and our dreams eventually die. What you need to do after you have set your goals is desire to make them happen. The burning desire in you is what will make it a reality.

Don't listen to that voice in your head that's bringing in all the negativity; *"You can't do it, it's too hard, don't even try it, etc."* These are all mental obstacles. They're in your head, not a reality. The size of your thinking is a key factor in determining the size of your results. If you think BIG, then your results have to be big. If you think small, you limit yourself to small results. It's all up to you. No one controls your thoughts but you, be it good or bad. If your thoughts or ideas are bad, maybe it's time to change who you are. Maybe it's time to work on bettering yourself, and then working on something that's bigger and better than you are.

One of my favorite quotes is, *"Watch your Thoughts, they become Words. Watch your Words, they become Actions. Watch your Actions, they become Habits. Watch you Habits, they become Character. Watch your Character, they become Destiny"* -Patrick Overton.

You need to change your attitude, and think differently in order for your dreams to come true. You have to start changing the person within you first and then going after your dreams and goals would be much easier.

Stop the excuses and get results. Everyone has excuses, but those excuses don't have to stop them. At one time while I was studying for the LSATs, I thought that after taking several tests I was wasting my time, and I would not pass, for it was too difficult. It was then my sister Maryem insisted that I take the LSATs and see what happens. I took the LSATs and alhamdulillaah (All Praise belongs to Allaah (SWT) I passed with okay scores, and got into law school. It might have not been the best law school, but I got in. It was then I changed my mind and decided against it. I just continued with my MBA and decided that I would work on a PhD afterwards. The point of the story is don't let yourself stop you from becoming who you want to be.

It was my choice not to go to law school, but it felt good to get in, and accomplish my goal of getting in. I am very happy with the choices I have made, and the goals I have set for myself. I constantly re-evaluate my goals, and check off the ones I complete, and add new ones to the list. It keeps me alive and more energized than ever.

Many studies show that those who set up goals are much more successful in achieving their dreams versus those who never even take the time to write them down. What writing the goals down does is it ingrains the outcome we want. A few people who became successful with the goals they had were all of the Prophets of Allaah (SWT), especially Prophet Muhammad (PBUH), Dr. Bilal Philips, and Mubarakah Ibrahim. At any one time all of these people could have quit, yet they didn't. What makes them different than everyone else is their vision, and their strong passion. They all had four characteristics in common that led them to success: 1. Optimism 2. Cheerfulness 3. Creativity 4. Perseverance (the ability to overcome obstacles).

Prophet Muhammad (PBUH) had a message to take to the people from Allaah (SWT). His mission was strong and his message was clear; *"There's Only One God."* At one time his uncle came and wanted him to give up this religion he was pursuing. The Prophet (PBUH) said, *"If you gave me the moon in one hand, and the sun in the other hand, I would not give up my religion."* He (PBUH) knew his mission, and he was very successful with it. Today, Islam is the fastest growing religion in the world. Here are some people who agree and attest to that:

"Islam is the fastest-growing religion in America, a guide and pillar of stability for many of our people..."

-HILLARY RODMAN CLINTON, Los Angeles Times, May 31, 1996, p.3

"Already more than a billion-people strong, Islam is the world's fastest-growing religion."

-ABC NEWS, Abcnews.com

"Islam is the fastest-growing religion in the country."

-NEWSDAY, March 7, 1989, p.4

"Islam is the fastest-growing religion in the United States..."

-NEW YORK TIMES, Feb 21, 1989, p.1

"Moslems are the world's fastest-growing group..."

-USA TODAY, The population reference bureau, Feb. 17, 1989, p.4A

"Muhammad is the most successful of all Prophets and religious personalities."

-Encyclopedia Britannica

"There are more Muslims in North America than Jews now."

-Dan Rathers, CBS NEWS

"Islam is the fastest growing religion in North America."

-TIME MAGAZINE

"Islam continues to grow in America and no one can doubt that!"

-CNN, December 15, 1995

"The religion of Islam is growing faster than any other religion in the world."

-MIKE WALLACE, 60 MINUTES

"Five to 6 million strong, Muslims in America already outnumber Presbyterians, Episcopalians, and Mormons, and they are more numerous than Quakers, Unitarians, Seventh-day Adventists, Mennonites, Jehovah's Witnesses, and Christian Scientists, combined. Many demographers say Islam

has overtaken Judaism as the country's second-most commonly practiced religion; others say it is in the passing lane."

-JOHAN BLANK, US NEWS (7/20/98)

"In fact, religion experts say Islam is the second-largest religion in the United States ... Islam has 5 million to 6 million members, followed by Judaism, with approximately 4.5 million ... And Islam is believed to be the fastest-growing religion in the country, with half its expansion coming from new immigrants and the other half from conversions."

-ELSA C. ARNETT, Knight-Ridder News Service

You can be a poor person growing up in the hoods of New York, or a bilingual who just came from another country. If you possess the correct skills anyone could be a success. All you need is a burning desire to succeed, and a dream to start your mission. I love teaching youth and adults these skills, for I think it can help save their lives a lot of times and open opportunities for them like they never expected.

What is it that you want to achieve?

Exercises

Exercises I would like you to do: Make a list of 10 goals and put deadlines by each goal, if possible. Next, work on the first five goals, ones that you can accomplish immediately. For example, start walking twenty minutes a day, three times a week. Start eating healthy as of tomorrow. Start reading ten minutes every night, as of tonight, etc. By setting goals, you are searching within yourself to seek what has to get done, and how you will do it. As you're doing this, you will start to realize some of your dreams, and the importance of them. No dream is too big. Write down all of your goals and dreams. People who write down their goals are much closer to achieving their goals. They can see clearer what it is they want. Once you can visualize, then you can start writing steps on how to achieve those goals.

10 Goals and Deadlines:

1--

2--

3--

4--

5--

6--

7--

8--

9--

10---

Step 6:

Business Plans

It had been several days since Wali and Zeba had begun thinking of different ideas and ways to get a business started. They both had many ways of doing something that was creative and different, but like everyone else who was new to the business world, they had many questions about the process.

The ideas were the easiest part of the equation, as Zeba saw it. It was the how-to of the business that worried her more than Wali. He had thought about some of those questions, and planned to discuss them with Zeba at their next meeting.

The days seemed to fly by. For this occasion, Wali and Zeba decided to meet on the porch outside. The weather had been nice and the porch was clean and they could enjoy the fresh air. Zeba was there first and reviewing her notes when Wali joined her.

"Assalaamu-alaykum, Zeba," Wali said.

She replied, "Wa-alaykum assalaam, Wali."

"Are you ready for the big plan?" Wali asked.

"I'm ready, but I also have a million questions," Zeba said.

Wali smiled and hoped that he could help her resolve as many questions as possible, so they could move on to the next step of the project. "Okay, let's get started. What ideas did you come up with for our business plan?"

"I came up with many ideas. Insha'Allaah, we can talk about which ones will work for us. The first one I want to speak about is, inventing a potato peeler. I had in mind, basically, a little machine that, when you throw potatoes in, it peels them for you."

"I think that is an excellent idea," Wali said, "but, unfortunately, someone beat you to it. There already is a potato-peeling machine."

"Oh, I didn't know that," she said, chagrined.

"Never mind, it was a good idea, and it shows that you are thinking along good lines. What else did you come up with?"

"The next item on my list is one that I think everyone could use: an iron that irons clothes itself, kind of like a robot for ironing. You put, say, ten items on hangers and give them to the robot and let it iron the clothes for you. As I have imagined it, it would feel the cloth to know what degree it should iron it so that it doesn't burn it, and I think maybe you could somehow program in what the piece of clothing was — a shirt, for instance." She looked with a question at her brother. "Has someone already invented that?"

"Not that I have heard," he said. "What else?"

"Lastly, I want to make a talking-interactive computer. By that I mean a computer that you speak to and tell it to do certain tasks, and it follows directions. This would be especially good for the elderly or the disabled, or even for people who don't know how to use a computer. They would still be able to navigate the internet, get papers written, résumés done, listen to news, watch broadcasts, and all the other things that one uses a computer for." Zeba looked at Wali for approval.

Wali had listened attentively to Zeba's suggestions. He was surprised at his sister's level of intelligence. He noticed again that she was brighter than other kids her age, and wondered how much this had to do with her being home schooled. Most children her age were in the eighth grade, but she was already in the tenth. Of course, he knew too that much of it was simply Zeba's willingness to apply her knowledge right away.

"Those ideas are all wonderful, even the potato peeler," he said. "I am proud of you."

"But now I want to hear your ideas," she said, pleased by her brother's compliments.

"Well, like you I had many ideas, but I only wrote a few down," he said. "The first one I thought of was a robot that takes care of farms. So if we were to make ten robots and gave them instructions on what to do, they would do all the labor on the farm, without getting tired. Basically, it would be a matter of programming the robots to perform the different chores.

"The second idea that I came up with is a car that drives based on the driver's speaking to it. You talk, and the car drives. My third idea is to have a robot teacher who can teach kids at home. All you have to do is put in a disc for what grade you want the robot to teach, and the lessons begin." Wali stopped there and looked at Zeba for feedback. "Well what do you think?"

Zeba smiled. She was fascinated by his ideas. They were so cool. "They are wonderful ideas. So, now we have six great ideas between us — no, only five without the potato peeler. Which one of the five will we choose? How should we pick?"

Wali thought for a few minutes. "I know, we can write down everything that is needed to make each one of these ideas work, and then pick the idea that has a massive market and would still be a great invention. What do you think?"

"That's perfect. Let's get to it right now."

"Let's each of us make another list," Wali said. "Put a line down the middle, and write down all the benefits on one side of the page, and all the faults and risks on the other."

They had spent about an hour on this when they heard the adhaan. They both instantly stopped everything they were doing and made the du'aa one reads after the adhaan, and got ready to pray.

Their parents knew by now that their children were up to something. They just smiled, and thanked Allaah (SWT) for everything they were blessed with, especially their son and daughter. They had wanted to have more children, but were unable to. Now they couldn't imagine their lives without these two.

Ten minutes later, Wali and Zeba were both back in the room. "Wali, I am done with my list," Zeba said. "How much longer do you need?"

Wali looked up, and thought for a moment, and said, "Give me another ten minutes."

Zeba nodded, and got up to check on her grandma and grandpa. About ten minutes later, she came back into the room. Wali was just reviewing his notes, and looked up.

"I'm ready, let's get started," he said. "After lots of thinking and list making, it seems to me that the best idea of them all is the talking-interactive computer. What about you, Zeba? What is your first business choice we should work on?"

Zeba looked at her notes. "I came up with the talking-interactive computer as my first choice as well. I'm sure I could come up with a prototype for one, pictures, ideal model, and the like. I would love to work on those parts."

Wali had a big grin on his face. "Great. I will work on the inside of the computer, the necessary tools it needs to make this talking-interactive computer become a reality. I will also work on getting a business plan done for our project. Most importantly, I will get in touch with all the big computer companies, to see who would like to buy this idea from us once we have it developed."

Wali and Zeba looked at one another. Both of them wondered if this could really be happening. They were amazed at how it was all coming together, their heads filled with millions of different ideas.

"It is astonishing, isn't it, how this has developed," Wali said, thinking aloud. "We started by reading books. Once we were inspired, we began with our own ideas and creativity, and now we might be looking at one of those ideas taking shape. Can you believe it, Zeba?"

Their grandmother interrupted them then, calling for Zeba to help her cook her famous kabob dish.

"We'll need at least several months for this part of our project," Wali said. "It's important that we continue to work at it and believe in it and ourselves."

"I will enjoy this part of the project," Zeba said. "It's fun to see something take shape."

"Meanwhile," Wali said as they both left to do their chores, "we'll meet every week to get an update to see how far we have each come."

"You may have the loftiest goals, the highest ideals, the noblest dreams, but remember this: nothing works unless you do."
Nido Qqbein

What is a Business Plan? A **business plan** is a formal statement of a set of business goals, the reasons why they are believed attainable, and the plan for reaching those goals. It may also contain background information about the organization or team attempting to reach those goals (www.wikipedia.org).

Business plans are important to focus on for financial goals or service goals, depending on if it's a profit or non-profit business.

Business plans can also be marketing plans. They can help figure out things one did not know before working on the business plan. I have used my business plans primarily as decision-making tools.

Three Types of Business Plans

1 **"Elevator Pitch."** This tends to be the shortest business plan, about two-three minutes long. This business plan is often used to awaken the interest of people, especially customers, strategic partners, and potential funders.

2 **Oral Presentation.** This could include a PowerPoint, and an oral narrative to trigger discussion and interest for possible investors to read the written presentation.

3 **Written Presentation.** It is usually detailed and written well.

Here is what a generic business plan structure looks like:

* Executive Summary
  1. Highlights
  2. Objectives
  3. Mission
* Company Summary

- Services
- Market Analysis Summary
- Strategy and Implementation Summary
- Management Summary
- Financial Plan

I have provided an example of a business plan as a guideline. The business plan is from the website: http://www.bplans.com/sample_business_plans/Car_Wash_And_Automotive_Business_Plans/Car_Wash_Business_Plan/executive_summary.cfm

Executive Summary

1.0 Executive Summary

Soapy Rides is a prominent hand car wash serving East Meadow, Long Island, New York. Mark Deshpande, of the prominent Deshpande family runs Soapy Rides. The Deshpande family has been serving the Long Island area with a car repair business and property development/management for over 30 years. Mark will be leveraging the incredible good will and brand recognition of the Deshpande family name to quickly gain market penetration.

The Business

Soapy Rides will provide customers with three services: exterior car washing, interior cleaning, and detailing. Soapy Rides has no true competitors trying to offer a high quality service at a reasonable rate. Most are trying to compete on price alone. Soapy Rides' ability to provide a high quality service, both in regards to the actual washing as well as customer service is all based on their ability to find the best employees. Hiring the best employees is cost-effective because it decreases HR costs associated with turnover and other employee costs. Hiring the best employees and making sure that they are well taken care of ensures that they in turn take care of the customers. Study after study proves that a happy employee is far more likely to provide the highest level of customer service compared to an employee who is not happy and feels that they are being taken advantage of.

The Customers

Soapy Rides will target three main groups of customers: individual car owner and leasers, car dealerships, and local businesses. The surrounding area is quite affluent, 40% of the residents earn over $70,000 a year. Consequently, they have nice cars and want them to look nice. There are five different car dealerships within a three-mile radius, which will require car-washing services for the various fleets. Lastly, there are many different local businesses that have company cars and that require clean appearances.

The Management

The strength of Mr. Deshpande's experience and his family's name equity and assistance, is Soapy Rides' competitive edge as well as a significant asset. Mark has been involved in the family's car repair business for the last ten years. He has worked his way through the organization and has been the manager for the last five years overseeing operations of $1.2 million annually. Before the family venture, Mark received his MBA from Cornell University. With 30 years invested in the community, the Deshpande family name has generated significant value as a fair, active member of the community. Lastly, Soapy Rides will be able to leverage several of the Deshpande's for their business expertise.

Soapy Rides is positioning itself as the premier hand car wash serving the Long Island area. Mark has forecasted a 20% market share. The business will generate a 95% gross margin and an 11% net margin after year one and 20.79% after year three. By year three the business will have developed a yearly net profit of $48,000.

Highlights

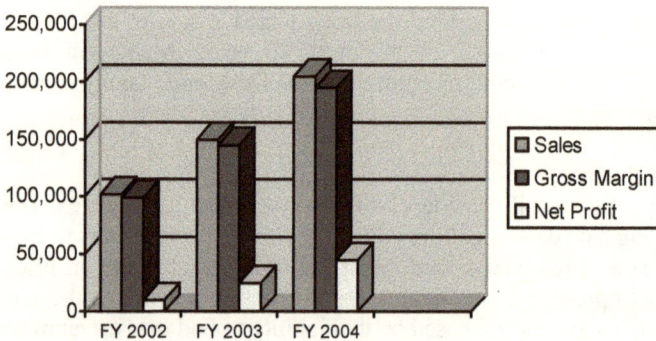

1.1 Objectives

The objectives for Soapy Rides Car Wash and Detail Service are:
To be viewed as a premium car wash and detail service in East Meadow.
Maintain a gross profit margin of over 95%.
Maintain a net profit margin of 10-15%.
Expand to two locations after third year of operation.

1.2 Mission

The mission of Soapy Ride is to provide top-quality washing and detail service for luxury car owners in East Meadow, NY. Soapy Rides will work to keep employees satisfied in order to maintain impeccable customer service.

I would advise you to look at this website for more samples of business plans: http://www.bplans.com/Sample_Business_Plans/all_plans.cfm.

How Can One Prepare a Business Plan?

One can do it themselves or hire someone to do it. If you don't have a lot of money to start with, I would advise doing it yourself. If you have some money to spend, I would still advise doing the rough draft of the business plan yourself, and then hiring someone to give it a more professional look.

If you're looking to hire someone I would say there are several resources you can find on the web to use. They have great testimonials:

www.MasterPlans.com

www.businessplans.com

www.dtcapitalinc.com

Some common mistakes people make with their business plans are:

1. They put it off: Until it becomes a must, they don't even work on it. This could be deadly to them, for if they had a business plan, they could have avoided many mistakes. They're too busy, and think they don't need it right now.

2. Fear and dread: They fear it will be very difficult to do. They're dreading the process of putting it together. Because they're afraid they don't do it.

3. Thinking one size fits all: Each business plan is different from other plans, just as each human being is different from other humans. Only the person with the mission can know how to make his business plan. Don't just throw anything in the plan, be clear and concise.

Exercises

Exercises that I want you to work on for your business plan:

By now, most of you have a vision of what you want to do, and how you want to start it. Whether you know what you want or not, I would suggest going to this website and looking through all the sample business plans, and envision your own business plan among them:

http://www.bplans.com/Sample_Business_Plans/all_plans.cfm

I would then just start writing a sample business plan. This could take you 20 minutes or longer.

Last, have someone check out your sample business plan. This could be your million dollar project you put together in minutes. One idea is all it takes.

Write a Simple Business Plan:

Step 7:

Finding Funding

Three months flew by, and it was time for Wali and Zeba to meet again. They had worked hard on their individual parts of the project, and by now both of them knew that this wasn't as easy as it might have seemed at the beginning. They decided, however, they would simply do the best they could, and continue from there if things weren't perfect, especially since this was their first experiment on such a big project. They had each made many things in the past, and both were very creative, but their past accomplishments were nothing compared to this.

They decided to meet after Fajr prayer, at what had become their usual meeting spot in the attic. They would each bring all of the stuff they had worked on, and figure out what the next step would be. Both of them carried lots of stuff in their bags when they met. They sat down and spread everything out on the floor between them. There was no furniture in the attic, but it was big and carpeted.

Wali began their meeting: "Well, how did you do? Did you get everything done?"

Zeba laughed and shook her head. "Not completely, Wali. I have the prototype and the pictures. The model was too difficult to make; insha'Allaah I can make it by the next meeting." She then showed Wali the pictures and the prototype that she thought would be perfect for a talking-interactive computer.

Wali looked over them and liked what he saw. "There is always room for improvement," he said, "but for a first try I'd say it's pretty good."

It was his turn then to share what he had done. "I was able to order all the parts which I needed from a website on-line and I've been working at creating an interactive computer," he said. "I also made a twenty-page business plan outlining what we are doing and where we want to go, and I wrote a mission statement for us. You are more than welcome to revise it, if you think it needs revision.

"The best news, though, is that I got in touch with Microsoft, and it turns out they might be interested in working on this project with us. They have been thinking about putting together something similar, but the project has been sitting on the shelf for a year or more. They said if we can actually come up with a model that is able to show them what we want it to do, then they might buy the whole idea and model from us. Zeba, that means, we could become millionaires instantly!"

"Are you serious? Wow! I never imagined that happening so fast! Mom and Dad will be so happy with us, and Grandma and Grandpa too! SubhaanAllaah. We can help our family, help the orphans, and feed the poor — everything we planned."

Wali had his own thoughts about how great this project could be. One of the important considerations in his mind was that it could be exactly what he needed to get into Yale.

"We have one small problem, though," he told Zeba. "We need money to be able to develop this project further. We also need to talk to some experts, and get more ideas for actually setting this interactive computer up. All of this could cost us anywhere from ten thousand to thirty thousand dollars, and that's if we're thrifty. Where can we get money like that to help us jump-start our new venture? We also have to remember, if it is not a success, we just lost that much money."

Zeba considered what he'd said. "Maybe we can ask Uncle Zakariya to help us out," she suggested, "and then we can pay him back once we get our money. He is rich, and I'm sure he would be pleased with our doing something big like this. He's always telling us to learn more about business, and that business is the key to financial freedom. What do you think, Wali?"

Wali loved the idea. Zeba was right, Uncle Zakariya would be supportive of a project like this. They might even let him help put this transaction together with them. Uncle Zakariya was a businessman himself, and that way they could learn from him as well.

"That's a great idea," he said enthusiastically, "but let's do one additional thing. Let's take a few days and each make a list of five different ways we might be able to get this project funded. That way together we will have a list of ten possible means to make our project work. Meanwhile we can still work on the interactive computer as well. Let's meet up next Thursday after Fajr prayer."

Zeba agreed. This was getting so exciting for both of them. They were starting to see a vision they had never seen before. Things were actually falling into place. They knew things wouldn't always be so smooth, but they were strong and weren't going to give up.

Wali and Zeba had been close to each other since their childhood. They weren't like other siblings who bickered and teased one another. They had learned early on to respect one another. Maybe it was the way they had been raised. The family never yelled or screamed or hit one another, so they were not exposed to those types of behaviors, therefore they did not learn to behave that way. They couldn't understand why so many kids their age were rude and disrespectful to their parents and other adults. They knew they were fortunate to have the blessings of Allaah (SWT) with them.

Wali and Zeba each went their own way to work on this big project, both more excited than ever — and each had, too, their own fears about things going wrong in the process. They had agreed, though, that they would trust in Allaah (SWT) to show them if what they were doing was a good thing or not.

"We now accept the fact that learning is a lifelong process of keeping abreast of change. And the most pressing task is to teach people how to learn."
Peter Drucker

What is funding? Funding is the ability to provide money for a project, a person, or a business. It could be a private or public institution. Two ways that I suggest to get funding are to look for private investors or grants. Both are available depending on what one is doing. If you have a great idea or invention, you might look for someone who is more of an investor, to help invest in your product, service or idea. If one is working on a non-profit, then they can help fund it by grants. We will discuss more of this in detail in the next two paragraphs.

Where can one find investors? There are many investors out there today. One has to just keep networking, and he or she will be able to connect to the correct people. There are many people out there who have money, and yet no idea of what to do with it. So the person with the service, idea, or product needs to connect with an investor who can see the same vision. This could take some time; one just has to be patient. A great example of this would be Colonel Sanders.

In 1955, when Colonel Harland Sanders retired at the age of 65, he had little to show for himself except an old Caddie roadster, a $105 monthly pension check — and a recipe for chicken. Knowing he couldn't live on his pension, he took his chicken recipe in hand, got behind the wheel of his wagon, and set out to make his fortune.

His first plan was to sell his chicken recipe to restaurant owners, who would in turn give him a residual for every piece of chicken they sold — five cents per chicken. The first restaurant that he called rejected him. He made many more calls after that, and they all rejected him.

In fact, the first 1,000 sales calls Colonel Sanders made ended in rejection. Still, he continued to call on owners as he traveled across the USA, sleeping in his car to save money. Prospect number 1009 finally gave him his first "yes."

After two years of making daily calls he had signed up a total of five restaurants. Still the Colonel pressed on knowing that he had a great chicken recipe and that someday the idea would catch on.

Five restaurants was nothing for two years' worth of work, but he knew he had something, and he didn't give up. By 1963 the Colonel had 600 restaurants across the country selling his secret recipe of Kentucky Fried Chicken (with eleven herbs and spices).

Colonel Sanders started off with selling his recipe and progressed to being part of a big franchise. He could not have gotten from one place to the next or retired as a millionaire if he hadn't started somewhere. He began with one small idea, which took him a thousand different directions.

Imagine yourself at the age of 65, having only so much money to live off. What would you do? I can tell you from research that most people would just take the pension check, and maybe work part-time. Some people at the age of 65 are still working to make ends meet. How I wish I could tell them to "make something happen." Do something. Work on a project or idea, and be passionate about it. Just don't give up.

I hope this story encourages you to believe in your dream at any cost. If your dream is strong enough, then you will find a way to make it happen.

Another way that one can fund their product, service, or idea is through their own savings. My next question to you is, have you saved any money? That would be a great way to invest in you. If you have saved for a rainy day, this would be the day to start using it.

Working and then saving as much as you can is another way to save for your product, service, or idea. This way is also a great way; one can make their dreams happen. This way also ensures that one does not get into debt.

What is a grant? A grant is defined as a giving of funds for a specific purpose. Many examples of grants are: opening up schools, hospitals, organizations to help kids, and organizations to help battered women. While one is pursuing their passion, they are also able to get paid for their work. There is so much one can do in this arena, it's amazing.

Grants will all depend on the type of organization that it is. You can research the web, and many others places and find out more about grants. A great resource I would recommend is:

http://www.americorps.org/

I would also talk to a grant writer about your project. They are experienced and know what to look for. They can also help one achieve their goals much faster.

Fellowships are another way to get free funding. Fellowships are grants for postgraduate study, research or work placements. They are usually awarded to graduate students based on the applicant's academic excellence. This allows one who is studying to do what they love to do, meanwhile get paid while working on that project.

There are also project grants available out there. As surprising as it is, there are many people willing to support different types of projects.

Venture Capital

Venture capital is a type of private capital usually provided by professional, outside investors to new, growing businesses. Investors usually give cash in exchange for shares in the company that is being produced. Venture capitals can be high risk; therefore they receive high returns on their investments. The one negative effect of venture capital is that venture capitalists get to have a say in the company decisions.

I would like to share with you two stories at this time, to make this information more understandable.

The first story is about a venture capital that was very successful. It is the story of www.Google.com.

"Google began as a research project in January 1996 by Larry Page and Sergey Brin, two PhD students at Stanford University, California. They hypothesized that a search engine that analyzed the relationships between websites would produce better results than existing techniques, which essentially ranked results according to the number of times the search term appeared on a page" (www.wikipedia.org).

These two guys were able to get $100,000 to start their venture from Andy Bechtolsheim, in 1997. "Google's initial public offering took place on August 19, 2004. 19,605,052 shares were offered at a price of $85 per share. Of that, 14,142,135 (another mathematical reference as v2 ˜ 1.4142135) were floated by Google and 5,462,917 by selling stockholders. The sale raised $1.67 billion, and gave Google a market capitalization of more than $23 billion. The vast majority of Google's 271 million shares remained under Google's control. Many of Google's employees became instant paper millionaires. Yahoo!, a competitor of Google, also benefited from the IPO because it owns 2.7 million shares of Google. Imagine going from being students to starting up a start up Computer Company to becoming billionaires. All of this happened in a matter of seven years.

Most people don't even get a raise of 25% in that amount of time; forget change the way they live forever. I feel there were two components to the success of the founders of Google. One was they were intelligent. They studied, and worked on their passion. The second was they took a risk and became entrepreneurs. They were passionate about their idea, and knew it would be successful. They believed in themselves, and then were able to win over many highly successful venture capitalists to invest in their company, including a competitor called Yahoo!. This is one of the best success stories of entrepreneurs using venture capitalists to help them gain success.

The next story is about Webvan.com, a business that started out strong and got many venture capitalists to invest in them, but went bankrupt in no time at all. Webvan.com was an online grocer that flopped. It went from one location to eight locations in no time. However, the grocery business has a very thin line of money-making margins, and it wasn't able to attract enough customers to justify the amount it was spending. In about 18 months it raised 375 million in IPO. It attracted more funding than any other company except Amazon.com. It had companies such as Softbank, Benchmark Capital, Sequoia Capital, and many more on its side. At one time their stocks were more than $30.00 a share, and in 2001, just two years later, stocks were selling for six cents a share. They were worth 1.2 billion at one time. Unfortunately, they spent about 1 billion of that on a gigantic infrastructure warehouse. The company closed as of July, 2001.

Islamic Finances

For all of those Muslims who have run out of ways to get financial help, there are always Islamic finances. Getting an Islamic loan to start off a business can be somewhat challenging, but is definitely worth a try.

Here are a few Islamic banks to call, and speak to about your situation: 1. Amana Mutual Funds Trust, 2. American Finance House, Lariba Bank, 3. MSI Financial Service Corporation, 4. Manzil USA. I would do a Google search for these places and contact them by phone, email, or letter.

The next resource for funding is getting private investors to invest in your business. There are many ways this can happen for you. Ask family and friends who know other people who might be interested. Lastly, connect with people through different network groups and sell your idea as Colonel Sanders did. One of those websites where you can connect to other investors is: goBIGnetwork.com/private-investor, www.privateinvestorsforum.com. There are many more websites like these. Just do a search on Google for private investors.

What is a joint venture? Joint venture is often abbreviated as JV. JV is an entity formed between two or more parties to work on a business together. The two parties have to agree to both put in money in this new business, and share in the expenses, revenues and the control of the business. Joint ventures are really **great** when two companies are working towards the same goals, or when two people want to accomplish the same business. This is **great** especially when one doesn't have enough funds to do it alone. It also brings more creativity to the table, and allows being stronger. Once one has their idea, service or product, then one can look for people who are in similar arenas as themselves. Some examples of this would be Cingular and SBC joining together, as well as Sony and Ericsson. Sony is a Japanese consumer electronics company, and Ericsson is a telecommunications company that makes mobile phones. Primarily the reason for this merger was to combine Sony's expertise to Ericsson's expertise so that they could be the leaders in their field.

Grocery stores join together all the time so they can lead in their industry. The main thing to remember with a joint venture is two people have to want the same results. They have to have the same goals. Then they will do whatever it takes to be successful.

Step 8:

Synergy

Thursday morning finally arrived. Wali and Zeba had been busy working on their project as well as preparing for their guests, who were coming on Saturday. They had decided to invite their Uncle Zakariya and his family over for dinner.

Their parents now knew something big was about to happen, although they had no clue what it could be. Wali and Zeba had offered them no explanation, but their parents went along with their plan to have Uncle Zakariya and his family to dinner, and waited to see if their children would say anything.

Wali and Zeba's lips remained sealed. They had discussed this question and had decided at their last meeting that they would tell their parents about what they are doing as soon as they had someone to help them fund the project. They wanted their parents to be proud of them. They would know at that time that Wali and Zeba were serious in what they wanted to do.

Uncle Zakariya lived a few hours away from them, in the small town of Carmel, California. He loved hearing from his nieces and nephews, and he was delighted when Wali called him, and excited when he heard that Wali wanted to speak to him about a business proposal.

Zakariya was very fond of Wali and Zeba. He knew they were both very intelligent and he was delighted to know that they were up to something. The idea that his favorite nephew and niece were in business pumped him up.

He sat for a moment after he had hung up the phone and thought about his own children. He wished they would think more like that. Sadly, he realized that was probably his own fault. He thought about the things he did for his children that were different from what Wali and Zeba's parents did for them. In retrospect, he wished he had not spoiled his children so much, and had given them more responsibilities.

There were so many things he wished he had done differently, but it was too late now to think about the past. He was still thankful for his children, and proud of them, but sometimes he wished they were more humble and grateful, and had the kind of initiative that Wali and Zeba were demonstrating.

"Who was on the phone?" his wife asked him.

"That was Wali and Zeba," he said with a happy smile. "They have invited us for dinner on Saturday. It seems they have a business proposition they want to go over with me."

"Alhamdulillaah, that's wonderful," his wife said, smiling as well. "I have missed them too and also the family. It will be a great visit to catch up, and talk about all that has happened, and the kids will be overjoyed. They love to be with their cousins."

* * * * *

Saturday came fast. Everyone worked very hard to prepare the dinner and clean the house. The drive was a long one, so Uncle Zakariya and his family were to stay overnight, which meant that bedrooms had to be gotten ready for them as well.

When the doorbell rang on Saturday afternoon, Wali and Zeba ran to open it. Wali got there first and greeted them, "Assalaamu-alaykum wa rahmat-Ullaahi wa barakaatuhu."

He saw that Uncle Zakariya had aged, and looked older than the last time Wali had seen him. Could this be due to stress from working so hard, he wondered? But he was still happy, at least.

"Wa-alaykum assalaam wa rahmat-Ullaahi wa barakaatuhu!" Uncle Zakariya said, and everyone else chorused it in the background. In no time, everyone was talking cheerfully to one another, often many of them talking at the same time in a happy din.

Finally Uncle Zakariya couldn't contain his excitement anymore. He approached Wali and asked the big question: "Wali don't keep me in suspense, what is this big business proposal you have for me?"

Wali smiled shyly and humbled himself. "Give me just a minute, and I will collect my materials, and call Zeba in and we will both present it to you in my room. Would it be possible if we had this as a private session with just you and us?"

Uncle Zakariya smiled. "Absolutely, I will be there in a few minutes. Let me just finish up my chai."

Wali nodded and called Zeba over. Zeba excused herself from her conversation with her aunt and her cousins and told them she would be back shortly. She and Wali hurried up to his room to begin organizing their presentation.

They had just finished setting everything up when Uncle Zakariya came in. He looked at what was before him with real curiosity. It seemed interesting. He wasn't quite sure what he thought it was, but he liked what he saw. Whatever it was, he could see they had obviously put a lot of time and effort into it.

"Alhamdulillaah. This looks great. But what am I looking at?" he asked.

Wali looked at Zeba for approval to begin and Zeba nodded. Wali began, "It is a talking-interactive computer that we have put together. I have already spoken to Microsoft, and they are interested in what we're doing. If we can get it to do what we want it to do, and patent it, they will buy it from us. As you can imagine, this is a new technology we're working on. We have done a lot thus far but there's still a lot more that has to be done in order for it to work the way we want it to."

He paused and looked his Uncle directly in the eyes. "That is where we are stuck. We have found many people who can help us launch this project, but we need some seed money to get it going. And that's where you come in, my dearest Uncle. We want to borrow some money from you, and then give it back to you once we sell our technology. This is not a gift we are asking for, however, it would be like you are investing in us. I have a business plan all ready to share with you, and projections of what I think this will cost us, and also what we should be able to get for it. Are there any questions you would like to ask us?"

Uncle Zakariya was amazed at what he had just heard. He had always known that Wali and Zeba were bright kids, but he'd had no idea how very intelligent they were. He smiled, and said, "Wow! How did you two come up with something like this? What triggered it? Whose idea was it? Most importantly how much do you need?"

Wali looked at Zeba, and nodded for her to take over the floor now. Zeba began, "As to how we came up with this idea, it was easy. We put our ideas in a pool, and picked this as the best one."

"But how did you come up with the first idea, to start a business?" Uncle Zakariya asked.

"That was triggered by many of the books we read. The most amazing one was 'The Greatest Salesman in the World'."

Uncle Zakariya nodded. He knew the book very well. He had read it many times himself.

"We need about thirty thousand dollars," Wali concluded.

Uncle Zakariya took a moment to consider that. Thirty thousand dollars wasn't too much for him. However, he knew that later they might ask for more, so he thought he should start them off with less and keep his budget open for up to thirty thousand when the time was right. He wanted Wali and Zeba to learn some lessons, and not just get the money without any struggles.

Zeba and Wali were eagerly waiting to see if he approved or not. He put his hand underneath his chin and grew serious. "This is very fascinating, and I like the idea," he said, "but thirty thousand dollars is a lot of money to invest in something as new as this. What if there are thirty other people doing the same as you two and one of them sells to Microsoft first. Then all of your hard work will go down the drain and my investment too."

He could see how disappointed they were, and he added quickly, "Don't get me wrong, you two are very bright and this is a worthy project, but there are risks with any business venture. I'll tell you what; I will invest ten thousand dollars in this project, to be repaid once this invention does succeed. If in the meantime, you get to a point where you are stuck and can't go any further without more money, then we will discuss the matter again at that time. Is this something you two are agreeable to?"

Wali and Zeba could no longer hold their excitement and ran to Uncle Zakariya and hugged him. "Yes, we'll take it. It's a deal!" they both shouted at once.

Wali's father heard the jumping and shouting and came to see what was going on. "What is happening in this room?" he asked, delighted to see all three of the people in the room looking so happy. "There seems to be a lot of joy and excitement here! Let me in on the secret!"

Wali looked at Zeba, and then his uncle. They both nodded to reassure Wali that the beans could be spilled.

"There's something we want to share with you," Wali told his dad. "Only, is it okay if we tell the whole family about it at once?"

"Absolutely," his dad said. "Let's go to the family room."

Each of them carried some part of the project downstairs and Wali began to set it up in the living room. The family noticed they were up to something and everyone quickly gathered around, asking what was going on.

Wali's dad said, "They're going to show us a project they are working on."

Wali and Zeba explained the project to the family and gave them a demonstration. Everyone loved it — everyone except one person: Uncle Zakariya's son, Rashad.

"It won't be possible," Rashad said harshly. "It's just a foolish dream."

The truth was Rashad was upset that his cousins were working on something great and that his dad was going to support them. Thus far in his own life he had accomplished exactly nothing, and he had all the resources he needed. He became very jealous.

"And I don't think it's a good idea for you to invest in this," he told his father. "The money will just be wasted. This will never succeed." Everyone became very quiet.

"That's enough," his father said sternly. "We'll change the subject now."

Wali and Zeba's mother hurried to serve dessert.

*"One mind working can be great, two minds working
can be extraordinary."*
Zohra Sarwari

Synergy is where two or more people come together for the same cause. Together they create an effect greater than they could alone. A great example is 1+1 = 11 and not two. Synergy creates that. When two great minds get together, they can produce magic. If you are in a mastermind group or hang around people who are making things happen, you will eventually start making things happen. Are the people that you hang around with important to your success? Absolutely! I strongly believe that your failures and success have a lot to do with who your associates are. The people around you affect the way you live your life and the way you envision the world.

Think about this for a moment. If your associates are negative, judgmental, angry people who always complain and backbite, will you be much different than them? In no time, you'll become like them. That's what you hang around with; their habits will become your habits. However, if you hang around positive, energetic, happy people who are always making things happen, eventually that will affect you as well. It's up to you to succeed or fail. Research shows that your income will be the average of the five people you hang around most with. Think about yourself; is that true?

"Your known by the company that you keep, so keep good company," Prophet Muhammad (PBUH).

Over and over it has been proven that those who are successful, be it in education, finances, marriage, or family, they have been in arenas where they were not only exposed to that, but they were taught those things, so they were successful with those things. Imagine if you hang around someone who is educated, do you think you will learn something? Better yet, imagine that you hang around someone who is religious, will you learn about religion? How about someone who is rich, will you become rich? This is vital to understanding this step.

If you are unhappy with how your life is at this time, then figure out what you are unhappy with, and start educating yourself in that area. The moment I realize I have a problem, I search for an answer by reading about people who had the same problems. I then search for the different ways they were able to solve their problems. By finding many ways to solve one problem, then I am able to tackle that problem at a higher level than when I first was faced with that problem. It's amazing what knowledge can do for us.

Yet, I cannot stress the importance of having good company; companions who are similar to you in many ways. People who have similar goals as you do. People who want to achieve greatness as you do. This is synergy. Hanging around those people once a week, can help your ideas, business, and success sky rocket. Constantly, I am searching for great people I can sit with; people who can help me as I can help them with their endeavors. People like that are difficult to find. Always look for people who are above you in knowledge and skill. Learn from them and raise the standards for yourself. It's never too late to begin. Only you can change you.

Exercises

Make a list of five people that you would love to learn from and increase your knowledge from:

1--

2--

3--

4--

5--

Step 9:

Balancing Your Life

Eight months passed. The talking-interactive computer was coming along well. Wali and Zeba had contacted many people from all over the world, some of whom were now working on the project with them for minimal costs. The project was nearing completion. They had only had to ask Uncle Zakariya for another seven thousand dollars, and that was it.

Finally, at the end of a year, the talking-interactive computer was finished. Wali and Zeba did another presentation for the family, and then asked Uncle Zakariya to go with them to present it to Microsoft.

By this time, even Rashad had a different attitude. At first, he had been entirely negative about this project, but after a while, he realized that it wasn't Wali or Zeba's fault that he felt so left behind in all this excitement. He could only blame himself, and no one else.

Having come to this realization, he went a step further and asked Wali about some of the great books that had inspired him and Zeba. Wali loved helping others and gladly gave his cousin a list, and also told him to call him anytime he needed anything. In no time at all, Rashad and Wali had become the best of friends.

* * * * *

The big day had come at last. Wali, Zeba and Uncle Zakariya sat in Microsoft's office. One of Microsoft's vice president came in and invited them into a meeting room, where they found several other employees assembled, waiting for them. Wali and Zeba were both very nervous, but they had discussed this at great length and they had already agreed that if it was meant to be, it would happen, and if it weren't, it would not happen. They left everything in the Hands of Allaah (SWT).

The presentation took several hours and the people in the room seemed to be very impressed with what they had seen. They asked many questions, which Wali and Zeba were able to answer clearly and concisely. At length, the vice president who had escorted them into the room told Wali, Zeba and Uncle Zakariya that he would take this project up with the board, and get back to them as soon as possible.

Two weeks later, the vice-president from Microsoft called to say he was authorized to offer a contract on this new invention and invited Wali and Zeba and Uncle Zakariya to come in the following day to discuss the terms of the contract.

Wali and Zeba found that they couldn't sleep that night for wondering what this invention of theirs could be worth to Microsoft. They decided simply to stay up instead and pray, thanking Allaah (SWT) for all the goodness that had been given to them.

The next day, they arrived at Microsoft filled with excitement. The entire family had insisted on coming as well, but the others waited outside in the car while Wali, Zeba and Uncle Zakariya went inside.

The meeting took about two hours. When Wali, Zeba and Uncle Zakariya came out of the Microsoft building their faces were expressionless, giving the family no clue as to what had transpired at their meeting.

Finally, when they were almost to the car, Dad couldn't stand the suspense any longer. He jumped out of the car and said, "Well, what's the verdict?"

Wali looked at Zeba and they both looked at Uncle Zakariya, and they all smiled at once. Wali said "We just sold the talking-interactive computer for 3.2 million dollars."

The others all jumped out of the car and danced around in delight, celebrating and crying, "Takbeer! Allaahu Akbar!" (Allaah is the Greatest!).

On the ride home, though, everyone was quiet, wrapped up in his or her own thoughts. They were each of them trying to imagine how this big check would affect them. All of them had one thought in common, however — how to use this money to help make the world a better place.

When they reached home, they all went into the dining room. Uncle Zakariya had brought his daf with him, and he fetched it now and began to play for them. An ancient part of Islamic tradition, the daf is a thin band of hardwood, covered on one side with goatskin.

Wali and Zeba, however, could only contain themselves so long, and after a time, they excused themselves and went to their rooms, the others smiling understandingly after them.

Zeba came to Wali's room with her list. "Wali, would you like to talk about what we are doing next?" she asked, all abeam.

Wali laughed, sharing his sister's excitement. "Yes, let's talk about our list of goals and then go to ask our parents and grandparents for their approval."

"The first thing we should do," Zeba said, "is give twenty percent of it away. I've already done the math. That is six hundred and forty thousand dollars. Which charities do you think we should help fund?"

Wali took a moment to think about this question. "I know," he said, "let's each write down five charities we want to give to, and we'll meet after lunch and discuss our choices."

During lunch, the family all waited to hear what Wali and Zeba had planned next. Finally, Uncle Zakariya asked the question that was on everyone's mind: "Well, children, what have you decided to do with your new money?"

Wali and Zeba looked at each other, and smiled. "Insha'Allaah," Wali said, "we will tell everyone later this evening what some of our plans are, and we hope then to get the approval of our elders."

The elders all knew that this wealth was a test that Allaah (SWT) had given the children, and in their heart of hearts each of them prayed that Wali and Zeba would pass this test. Wali and Zeba had asked at every prayer that, if they were to become wealthy, Allaah (SWT) would help them to pass that test, or else not make them wealthy at all. This was the beginning of their test.

After lunch, Wali and Zeba met again to compare the lists of charities that they had made.

"The first charity I want to give to," Zeba began, "is the mosque here in our own town. I want to make it possible for it to expand into a bigger building, so we have more room, and so they can have a special section just for kids. My second charity is to build an orphanage house in Afghanistan, the third charity is a shelter for abused women and children in our city, the fourth is to help build an Islamic private school in our community, and the fifth is to support the non-profit that delivers free meals to the elderly."

Wali once again was amazed by his sister's thought processes. He wondered how many kids her age would think the same way. "That's awesome, Zeba!" he said.

"What about your list?" she asked.

"Well, first I want to contribute about two hundred thousand each to ten different mosques that are being built in the US and elsewhere. Then I want to buy homes for our relatives in Afghanistan, and land so they can farm. It's still relatively cheap out there and we can help take care of our two aunts and their families and our grandparents, so that they will be self-sufficient. Third, I want to give to three different orphanages in three different parts of the world. Fourth, I want to help sponsor a program that takes care of the elderly in our community. And, finally, I want to start our own non-profit. I want to buy an old apartment complex, and renovate it, and allow people who are in dire need to stay there for free until they get themselves back on their feet. There would have to be some rules, of course. There would be a deadline of three to six months and in that time we would have to see them progressing and wanting to get out of the situation they are in. This would be primarily for people who are going through transitions in their life — for example, someone who lost his job or his home, or someone who just got divorced. We could work out something with different restaurants or markets for free food to cook at least one meal a day. Every month we can have a different contributor helping with this project, and we will have volunteers helping cook the meals, and doing other work, until we do well enough to hire employees. What do you think Zeba?"

Zeba had this awestruck expression on her face. "Wow, did you really think of all that?" she said. "That is amazing. I love it! And I think the family would love to be part of it as well. Our community definitely needs a place like this. Everyone runs into hard times and needs a little bit of help. This is wonderful! I think we need to speak to the elders now, so that we can divide up the money where it's needed and get started working on our plans."

Wali was so happy with giving away their money; he almost forgot what else he wanted to tell Zeba. "Zeba, I know we agreed to list five things each that we wanted to do with this money, but there is a sixth thing I want to discuss with you."

Zeba listened quietly to what he had to say. "Yes" she said when he was finished.

"After doing that for the sake of Allaah (SWT), I want to pay off a farm for our parents. They haven't been able to purchase one before because of the interest involved in borrowing money from a bank, but I want them to have it now, so they never have to worry about rent.

"And I want to put enough money away for them in a separate account," Wali added, "to pay for taxes and insurance for the house and their other expenses. They deserve that at the minimum. And once we do better with our businesses we can always add to their account."

"I want to put money away for Grandma and Grandpa, too," Zeba said, "in a separate account, should they need it for their health or anything else."

Zeba was in tears by now. She knew that Wali shared her desire to make sure their family was taken care of. She smiled through her tears and said "Don't forget we have to pay Uncle Zakariya, and look into tickets for Hajj for the whole family."

"We'll need to open different bank accounts for all these different projects," Wali said. "But for now, let's share our plans with the elders. After that, we can start to work on future business projects."

As they went down to rejoin the family, Wali and Zeba both knew that they were now ready to face the world, and to make a positive impact on it for the Sake of Allaah (SWT).

*"The most successful are those who
can balance their lives."*
Zohra Sarwari

Now that you have the formula to success, you have to figure out how to balance it. So much happens so fast, and you must decide which way to go first. So many people want to start off their businesses, services or ideas, that they put all of their time and effort in it. They keep telling themselves once they are successful, then they won't spend as much time working on their business. Research has shown this not to be really true. People want more and more and more. There is a hadith saying that, *"The son of Adam will never stop wanting more, until he is six feet under, and his mouth is full of dirt,"* Prophet Muhammad (PBUH).

What we need is balance in our lives. What is the definition of balance? Balance is when the soul, health and way of life are all in sync with one another. There must be a time to work and a time to have fun. There are different times for different activities.

The power of the soul! The soul can be defined as many things. In Islam, it is described in a hadith explaining to Muslims that the soul is established when Allaah (SWT) assigns an angel to "breathe" a soul into an embryo after 120 days of pregnancy. The soul is responsible for the good deeds of a person and can be interrupted by the devils which results in committing sin. In surah 15, verse 29 of the Qur'aan; the creation of man involves an angel of Allaah "breathing" a soul into him. This intangible part of an individual's existence is "pure" at birth and has the potential of growing and achieving nearness to God if the person leads a righteous life. At death the person's soul transitions to an eternal afterlife of bliss, peace and unending spiritual growth (Qur'aan 66:8, 39:20). This transition can be pleasant (Paradise) or unpleasant (Hell) depending on the degree to which a person has developed or destroyed his or her soul during life (Qur'aan 91:7-10).

It is believed that all living beings are divided into two parts: The physical (being the body) and the non-physical (being the soul). The soul is where activities like feelings and emotions, thoughts, conscious and sub-conscious desires and objectives take place. While the body, or physical actions, serves as a reflection of one's soul. That could be good or evil, either way it confirms what the intentions were.

There are many ways that we can ease our soul. One is to know truth, to know of our existence, and understand the reasoning behind it as best as we can. Next, is to understand that life will throw a lot of different situations at us, and if we have a calm soul we'll be able to handle all of those situations. Our soul will make sense according to the knowledge that we have obtained. In order for us to ever be happy, we have to be intrinsically happy first, and then in everything else that happens we'll feel joy.

If you haven't found out who you are, I would suggest soul searching for your reason of existence. "What is the purpose of life?" Once you can answer that question, then you're able to put everything else in perspective. Your mind will understand its position and start to make sense of your life. It will also know when to go into ease, and how to get into ease without effort; so all of those stressful situations and overwhelming days will know how to take care of themselves.

It is vital that one seeks knowledge other than that given to them. Balancing the soul is quite simple.

Once one gets into the habit of doing good deeds on a daily basis, then one's soul lightens up. Good deeds are many: smiling to anyone, listening to one who is distressed, feeding the poor, calling family to say "I love you," respecting your parents, siblings, and everyone else, etc. If you are interested in doing a good deed daily, and want to know what my recommendations for the day are, please email me at zohra@zohrasarwari.com, and request for the good deed daily lesson.

The second important part of balance is health. Health is vital to one's success. One has to take care of oneself. They have to eat healthy, and exercise daily. Exercise has been known to give one energy and vitality. It also helps prevent many diseases. I would recommend 20 minutes a day, 3 times a week. You could take a brisk walk, do a cardio exercise, ride your bike, take a jog, etc.

Without health we have nothing. Health is vital to our success. If we don't have energy then how can we achieve what we want? If we are too fat or too skinny and have issues with weight, can we focus on becoming great and achieving success? Therefore, we need to take care of ourselves mentally and physically. Physically we have to exercise several times a week, and always be active in everything we do. Turn off the television and go for a jog, and listen to a book on CD while doing it. You're killing two birds with one stone; you're getting knowledge and exercise at the same time. You can just go for a walk and let your mind rest. Sometimes the greatest ideas or thoughts come to me when I am going for a brisk walk. You can pick up a hobby like karate, tai chi, yoga, swimming, or any other sport, and do that sport several times a week. This will allow you to learn something new while getting exercise and resting your mind from the worries of the world. It will also allow you to become social with others, and expose them to what you are doing.

Health is a way of life, not something to toil with. Health needs to be seen that way, just as religion should be seen in that way. You don't practice health once a week and think that you will be healthy. Same with praying to the Creator, God the Greatest, you don't pray once a week. In Islam we pray five times a day. You should be eating the right foods always, and be changing your way of eating and exercise as if your life depended on it. Your life does depend on every choice that you make. You might not see the results of the choices you make today, but in the future you will. Imagine for a moment that you are eating **whatever you want**, you're not exercising, and you're doing **whatever you want**. It might seem to be the perfect life, but it has a lot of holes in it. In 10-20 years, you will have massive health problems, maybe obesity, diabetes, heart disease, or any number of other serious illnesses.

That's not a lifestyle to live by. That will be a sad way to live, and millions choose to live that way. Unfortunately, popping pills to help relieve pain for a short period of time begins to be the lifestyle of those people. Honestly, that is no way to live. Everything else starts being harmed including relationships due to the lifestyle one chooses. No one knows how long they will live; however, they do have a choice of how to live during that time span. No matter where you are on the scale of health, it's time to start thinking of goals to help you get where you want to go. If you want to change your lifestyle and become healthy and don't know where to begin, email me at zohra@zohrasarwari.com, and I will get some information from you and help you begin the process.

The third step to balance is getting your life organized. Your life consists of everything that is involved with your daily tasks. That includes school, work, family, activities, etc. Balancing your life has a lot to do with your soul and your health. If you have taken care of your soul and it is at ease, and have also started a routine for your health, as well as change the way that you eat, you have achieved 75% of the success to balancing your life. Now you have to organize your life by writing down what is most important to least important. Then you get an organizer and write down the most important things that have to get done daily. For example, exercise 30 minutes, read 20 minutes, pray 5 times, work 8 hours, do homework, have dinner with the family, do chores, and whatever else you need to get done in a day. Anything else should be considered a distraction, and tried to be avoided.

Once you can organize yourself to start thinking in that way, then you are able to have a much more fulfilled life. The reason we stress out so much is because we've piled things on our plate, and now we can't handle it. That can be true, therefore one needs to get organized and figure out what's necessary for them to grow and change, and what is not. You have to make those hard choices and let go of things that are not contributing to your success. For example, take time away from TV, music, gossiping, chatting nonsense on the phone, wasting time outside, reading gossiping magazines, reading books that won't help you grow, etc.

There are many things one can let go of, and find time for new and better things to replace their time with. Everything that you do on a daily basis, you should ask one question, "Is this benefiting me in any way?" If the answer is "no," then you need to stop doing those activities. In Islam many things benefit us. Listening to someone's problem, and helping them solve it in a good manner, is benefiting you in this world and the hereafter; cooking for a neighbor who is sick, is also going to benefit you in this world and the hereafter; taking care of your parents or siblings, will benefit you in this world and the hereafter. There are many things that might look like they're not benefiting us, but in reality they are. You just have to know what your values are first, to understand how it is benefiting you.

It is now that you can somewhat feel like life is starting to come together. Once you have that strong feeling of stability, then you're on your way to success.

Play

All work and no play can become a bore. Play is time that you can take for yourself. Everyone needs time to just relax their mind and reflect. So many of us are in a rush all the time and we never get any time for ourselves. For myself, my time is very limited, due to home schooling, and taking care of my children during the day. In the evenings, I get a few hours to write and work on my business. Then it's taking the kids to the park, dinner, etc. My day is finished.

Due to that I really have no time left to spend on me. What I have made time that is for me is waking up every morning when everyone else is asleep and praying to Allaah (SWT) as well as reading the Qur'aan. If I can get that daily dosage my day will be the best day. More time for me is praying 5 times a day, exercising 20 minutes every evening, and reading 30 minutes every night before bedtime. If I do those four things every day then I feel that I had my time to reflect and be at peace.

We each have a different definition of play; my definition of play when I was a youth was different than my definition of play now. Whatever is happening in your life, you need to remember to take some time away daily to reflect and relax. You have to fit playtime in, so that your mind can relax, and produce new information and ideas to help you with your present problems, or help you achieve solutions to what you are looking for. Without playtime, one will not be able to let everything go, and let new things in. Remember, even if you can give yourself only 20 minutes a day, do it. It will help you grow tremendously.

Play can help you be happy because for once you will focus on yourself and not everything else around you. It is these moments that make it worthwhile for one to see their vision and mission clearly.

The next topic that will be discussed is work. Work can have many meanings to different people. For the sake of argument, we will say work is when you are doing something that requires energy to get something in return.

If you are working for an employer, then you are doing what the job requires, and you are getting paid for it. If you are working for yourself, then you are doing things to help earn money for yourself. Work requires consuming energy that might make one too tired to do other things. I would suggest getting a job or working in a way where you can accomplish other tasks in your life as well. Too many people blame work for the inability to accomplish more in their lives. I'm telling you, if it is work that is limiting you to succeed, then you need to change your work, so that you can succeed.

Knowing that work can use a lot of energy, you might have to organize yourself where you can take care of important stuff early in the morning when you aren't tired. Once you are able to change your outlook on life, you'll be amazed at how much you can get done in a day. Your perspective on life leads to the way you live your life.

Google has done something great within their work environment. They allow 20% of their employee's time to go into some project that they want to work on. This allows them time for creativity. I feel everyone needs a day like that. Take one day a week and work on some project at work or on your business for fun. It is a lot of those projects that have made them millions thus far.

This brings me to the next topic of needing time to be creative. In order for us to continue growing and making changes, we have to have time to be creative. We have to take time away from our families to reflect and be creative with them, it is in those moments away we think of what we are doing right and wrong and how we can make things better. Even marriages need time away to focus, relax, and reflect — it is vital to one's success. We should have days out of the month to work on those categories we use most. One day off from work. One day away from children (if possible), one day away from our spouse (hang out with family or friends and reflect on all the good things that we have). I suggest these three categories to be most important, you can add your own categories as well. Imagine a whole day away from one area of your life that you use most. It might help develop that area much stronger. Also it will give you some peace of mind.

One thing to always remember about work or other things is to put 110% in everything that you do. So many people are not taught work ethics as children, and they grow up learning the hard way what work really is. It doesn't matter if you work for yourself or someone else. You have to have work ethics. Figuring out work ethics alone can help one succeed with many things in life. Not just work, home, family, but basically at all that one endeavors, put in 110% and give it the best you can.

I will just touch on a few work ethics that I feel are very important to one's success. The first one is to have a positive attitude. Attitude is everything. No matter what happens, smile, relax, and continue doing what you have to do. Don't waste your energy on being upset, or mad.

"Attitude is a small thing that makes a big difference" (Winston Churchill). It is easier said than done, you're probably thinking. You're right, but if we can work on it a little every day, then the possibilities are endless. We can start with certain areas in our lives that are easier to be positive about, then expand our horizons and work on deeper areas. For myself the hardest part of keeping my attitude positive is when I'm with my three little children. At times I feel upset or overwhelmed with all that they are doing wrong, but then I have to get myself back together and remember the importance of being patient and positive. I pray that Allaah (SWT) forgives me for getting impatient with my kids, and I pray that Allaah (SWT) gives me patience to be a better mom.

The next work ethic is to always be on time, even a few minutes early. This indicates that you care about your job and want to succeed. Timeliness is a key to success. Nobody likes one who is late or doesn't respect someone else's time. Once you can respect other people's time, you learn to respect your own time.

The last work ethic we will discuss is dependability. Being dependable is very important to one succeeding. By being dependable one is showing that they are committed to coming to work, and aren't lazy. It's in their character to do what's right. When one can imagine that if the tables were turned how they would feel, they know to do the right thing. When you are dependable, you are trustworthy and reliable. That speaks for itself. We need to work on our character daily to make it better. You are also responsible when you are dependable. There are many great qualities that come with being dependable.

Job Stresses That Keep Us From Having Balanced Lives

The first one that I want to discuss is not having enough income. That is a major stressor on lots of people. However, for every problem that exists, Allaah (SWT) has given us a solution. We just have to be wise and seek the solutions that best fit our lives. There are many ways to help release some of this stress. One of the best ways is to live below your means. Another way is to obtain a better job by getting more skills. You're thinking that's easy to say, yet hard to do. I beg to differ. If there's a will, there is a way. You can change your life with your attitude first, and then skill.

Always look to be more skillful, for the more you know and can contribute, the more you will be wanted. Don't do things just to get something in return. Do things because it's good to do; because you know it's the right thing to do. For Muslims, that means earning a good deed. Become good-natured, for that is the best way to be. Allaah (SWT) loves those with great characteristics and high morals.

One of the best ways to get paid more for what you do is to love your job and make improvements in it. The more you care about what you are doing, and the more you seek solutions to your job, the higher your rank can go, and eventually you will have a different job code. Remember, every good thing that you do will be rewarded to you one way or another.

Examples of People Who Are Well-Balanced

When I think of someone who is well-rounded, it has to be someone who has won respect in his home first, and then the outside world. So many leaders have won people's hearts and been able to influence many others. People write about them all the time, yet to me they are not the BEST leaders. If they cannot be a great husband, father, son, sibling, grandfather, cousin, etc., then why would I think they will be great with everyone else? Many people have double lives, and they think they are fooling the world. However, they are only fooling themselves.

A real leader, who is balanced in his life, is someone who can be respected inside his home as well as in public. Unfortunately, we are running out of those types of leaders by the minute. We are finding leaders that people respect and admire, but we have no idea how their home life is. For me to form an opinion of a person's ability to run the rest of the world, I need to see if he has the patience and perseverance for his family first, which can be extremely difficult.

The first example I will speak about is Prophet Muhammad (PBUH). He was a fine example for all mankind. From his great manners to the way he was with anyone he came in contact with, to his kindness to animals, the Prophet (PBUH) was one who was very generous and cared deeply for the poor. He had patience no one else had. History proves it over and over. Many people were witness to his attributes. He (PBUH) was a great leader, husband, father, friend, grandfather, and man. He was able to work, and yet not diminish his other roles. Many report he never yelled at children, and loved to give rather than to receive. He (PBUH) would feel disturbed if he'd received something and quickly didn't distribute it.

I have included some quotes about this great man who lived about 1400 years ago, and is still influencing over one billion people all over the world:

'Abu Dharr reported that one evening he was walking with Allaah's Messenger when he said,

"Abu Dharr, if the mountain of Uhud were turned into gold for me, I would not like three nights to pass and one dinar still be left with me, excepting what I would leave for paying my debts."'

'Abdullaah ibn Amr narrated:

"Allaah's Messenger (pbuh) neither spoke in an insulting manner nor did he ever speak evil intentionally. He used to say, "The most beloved to me among you is the one who has the best character and manners."'

(Recorded by Al-Bukhari)

'The Jews, in spite of their hostility to the Prophet (pbuh), were so impressed by his impartiality and sense of justice that they used to bring their cases to him, and he decided them according to Jewish law.'

[Abu Dawood]

'The Prophet (pbuh) not only preached to the people to show kindness to each other but also to all living souls. He forbade the practice of cutting tails and manes of horses, of branding animals at any soft spot, and of keeping horses saddled unnecessarily.'

[Sahih Muslim]

'If he saw any animal over-loaded or ill-fed he would pull up the owner and say, **"Fear Allaah in your treatment of animals."'**

[Abu Dawood]

'He stated, **"Verily, there is heavenly reward for every act of kindness done to a living animal."'** *Muhammad (pbuh) also used to command mercy for all animals such that they are fed well, watered well, not forced to carry too heavy a burden, and not tortured or maimed for one's enjoyment.*

Monopoly is unlawful in Islam and he preached that, *"It is difficult for a man laden with riches to climb the steep path that leads to bliss."*

He did not prohibit or discourage the acquisition of wealth but insisted that it be lawfully acquired by honest means and that a portion of it would go to the poor. He advised his followers,

"To give the laborer his wages before his perspiration dried up."

He did not encourage beggary either and stated that,

"Allaah is gracious to him who earns his living by his own labor, and that if a man begs to increase his property, Allaah will diminish it and whoever has food for the day, it is prohibited for him to beg."

Another person who has proven to have a well-balanced life is Anthony Robbins. Anthony Robbins is someone who is constantly mastering himself. He was a self-made millionaire at a young age, and has not stopped growing into being a better person. He has changed the lives of at least 50 million people all over the world, and is passionate about what he does. He is a man who tries to implement what he learns. Many people have great stories to tell. He has found many secrets to success, and is actually trying to help people find their success. Many people have been extremely successful in obtaining those successes. I see him as someone who is seeking truth, justice, and quality of life. I do not know him personally, but I do know he cares about people, and truly wants to help change people to be the best they can be. Although he is divorced one time, there are many great stories of him as a husband, father figure, and employer. Here are what some people say about Anthony Robbins:

"Tony Robbins has astonishing credibility. I have never seen a more powerful technology or a more powerful communicator. He walks his talk."

-Scott Degarmo, Editor-in-Chief, Success Magazine

"[He] provides an arsenal of tools for lasting change as well as lessons for enriching the quality of life. In fact, if enough people read his book and sincerely apply its teachings, it could put me and many of my colleagues out of business."

-Dr. Fred Covan, Head Psychologist, Bellevue Hospital, New York City

"Tony Robbins named one of the top 10 Outstanding People of the World."

-International Chamber of Commerce

The last step is learning how to put it all together. Children don't succeed if they get everything they want. They succeed when they are nourished and allowed to make their own choices. We have to support them, nourish them, and then allow them to become their own geniuses. This is vital to becoming successful. All of us are blessed with some type of genius. It is up to us to figure out what that is. We know ourselves better than anyone else. However, that doesn't mean that Satan doesn't take us down the wrong path and make us feel that is where our gift lies.

I see so many people who are crooks or hackers, and I think to myself, if they only used their intelligence and creativity in a great way, they would be so successful. They could be rich, smart, and successful. However, we all make choices. The choices you make early on, can affect your life greatly as you mature. Every choice we make has a cause and effect to it. We might not think so, but it does. Every choice we make as parents has a cause and effect upon what choices our children will make in the future. However, it is never too late to change and begin a new path.

I would like to share this quote with you again to help it stick in your memory:

'Watch Your Thoughts, They Become Words.
Watch Your Words, They Become Actions.
Watch Your Actions, They Become Habits.
Watch Your Habits, They Become Character.
Watch Your Character, They Become Destiny.'

– Patrick Overton

I try to live by these words. The moment a sad or mean thought comes to my mind, I stop myself by saying these words. It's amazing how quickly one can escalate in their feelings and ways when thoughts, change to words, to actions, to habits, to character, to destiny. Allaah (SWT) has blessed us with a mind so that we can use it to make wise decisions. Wisdom comes from knowledge and education. So many people are quick to judge without first researching and learning about why things may be as they are. Knowledge and education without action means nothing.

I see many people who are rich and poor, but who are not wise, because they don't research life to understand the purpose of it. They come up with decisions about their lives based upon what others have told them. They don't research to find out for themselves what the truth is. The truth is powerful. Sometimes people don't want to see the truth, for truth requires change. Change can be hard to accept. Without truth, it is difficult for one to have a stable foundation to build upon for success. What ends up happening is that they build their success on instability. Most problems take place when there is no stability.

This is why I started this book out with "Reading." Reading is what can help save us or hurt us, depending on what we read. It's vital when searching for the truth, to read materials that are not biased. It's important to read books that are empowering and could have a great effect on you. It is books like these that can change your life, and help you achieve greatness, but only if you have a stable foundation. I have tried to help people build success and achieve greatness, but because they did not have a stable foundation, they could not. Truth and stability is core to becoming successful. Many people build on the wrong foundation, and end up falling into many pieces. They are successful on the outside, but only Allaah (SWT) can see inside and knows the truth.

Next, we want to remember how important it is to start building your character. For those who believe in Allaah (SWT), God the Greatest, they were given guidance through the Prophets (PBUT), and books were revealed to them. In those Books, The Qur'aan, The Torah, and The Gospel of Jesus (PBUH), we are instructed and God the Greatest is guiding us towards the best character and morals. Also, the Messengers (PBUT) sent to the people, had the best qualities of character. We should actually imitate their great characters, for Allaah (SWT) chose them for a reason. For those who don't believe in God the Greatest, they should still read about the greatest messengers that existed, and at least learn from their characters, honesty, integrity, and other great qualities.

Now that you have built your foundation of truth, stability, and added some character blocks, you're ready to start thinking about being an entrepreneur. This step being somewhat difficult, your remembrance of failure has to be close to your heart. Without failure one cannot succeed in business. Remember, failure only means you have found many solutions that don't work, and you're still looking for the solution that will work for you. Due to time and market changes, one's success depends mainly on testing the waters, and figuring out what doesn't work in order to see what works.

You're becoming stronger and stronger. You're at a point in your life where you should start dreaming about what your purpose in life is. What are you meant to become, and how can it benefit society as a whole? Dream big, and write all your goals down. Start with small steps to work on your goals. Make deadlines to have your goals accomplished.

You are now ready for your business plan to be in the works. Start off the easy and free way, and get help as you're growing and getting established to become an entity by yourself.

With everything falling into place, now you want to figure out how to fund the project. Many different ways of finding funding was explained; explore your options. Make the best choice you can, and never stop seeking different ways to accomplish your goals. Try not to use interest as a means to help support your endeavor. It can bite you in the back and cause more harm than help.

Lastly, you have to be able to balance your life with all the new things that are occurring. We don't want you to fall apart at the height of success. We want you to flourish like a flower and bloom. Go over what is necessary to keep balanced as often as you can. For at times, even I need a reminder to take a break and let my mind rest. It's vital that break and exercise time is taken seriously, for it will be those times that will actually help you let creative thoughts out. If you work on these 9 habits and make them part of your life, your life is destined to change.

With that in mind, be strong and remember, become great, for great is what we are designed to be. It is that greatness that will help others. Don't think of only yourself; think of the rest of the world **YOU** can help change for the better **THEN YOU** become **Extraordinary.**

A Wise Young Boy

Many years ago, during the time of the Tabi'in (the generation of Muslims after the Sahaabah), Baghdad was a great city of Islam. In fact, it was the capital of the Islamic Empire and, because of the great number of scholars who lived there; it was the center of Islamic knowledge.

One day, the ruler of Rome at the time, sent an envoy to Baghdad with three challenges for the Muslims. When the messenger reached the city, he informed the khalifah that he had three questions, which he challenged the Muslims to answer.

The khalifah gathered together all the scholars of the city and the Roman messenger climbed upon a high platform and said, "I have come with three questions. If you answer them, then I will leave with you a great amount of wealth which I have brought from the king of Rome."

As for the questions, they were:

"What was there before Allaah?"
"In which direction does Allaah face?"
"What is Allaah engaged in at this moment?"

The great assemblies of people were silent. (Can you think of answers to these questions?)

In the midst of these brilliant scholars and students of Islam was a man looking on with his young son.

"O my dear father! I will answer him and silence him!" said the youth.
So the boy sought the permission of the khalif to give the answers and he was given the permission to do so.

The Roman came up to the young Muslim and addressed him, repeating his first question, "What was there before Allaah?"

The boy asked, "Do you know how to count?"

"Yes," said the man, slightly puzzled as to why he was asking such a strange question.

"Then count down from ten!"

So the Roman counted down, thinking that the young Muslim probably didn't understand. "Ten, nine, eight ..." until he reached "one" and he stopped counting.

"But what comes before 'one'?" asked the boy.

"There is nothing before one - that is it!" said the man.

"Well then, if there obviously is nothing before the arithmetic 'one', then how do you expect that there should be anything before the 'One' who is Absolute Truth, All-Eternal, Everlasting, the First, the Last, the Manifest and the Hidden?"

Now the man was surprised by this direct, intelligent answer, which he could not dispute.

So the Roman thought that he would do better with the second question. This young boy would surely not answer this question. "Then tell me, in which direction is Allaah facing?"

"Bring a candle and light it," said the boy, "and tell me in which direction the flame is facing."

"But the flame is just light - it spreads in each of the four directions, North, South, East and West. It does not face any one direction only," said the man in wonderment.

The boy cried, "Then if this physical light spreads in all four directions such that you cannot tell me which way it faces, then what do you expect of the Nur-us-Samawaati-wal-'Ard: Allaah - The Light of the Heavens and the Earth!? Light upon Light, Allaah faces all directions at all times."

The Roman was stupefied and astounded that here was a young child answering his challenges in such a way that he could not argue against the proofs! So, he desperately wanted to try his final question. He didn't want to be defeated by this young boy.

But before doing so, the boy said, "Wait! You are the one who is asking the questions and I am the one who is giving the answer to these challenges. It is only fair that you should come down to where I am standing and that I should go up where you are right now, in order that the answers may be heard as clearly as the questions."

This seemed reasonable to the Roman, so he came down from where he was standing and the boy ascended the platform. Then the man repeated his final challenge, "Tell me, what Allaah is doing at this moment?"

The boy proudly answered, "At this moment, when Allaah found upon this high platform a liar and mocker of Islam, He caused him to descend and brought him low. And as for the one who believed in the Oneness of Allaah, He raised him up and established the Truth. Every day He exercises (universal) power."

The Roman had nothing to say except to leave and return back to his country, defeated and ashamed.

Meanwhile, this young boy grew up to become one of the most famous scholars of Islam. Allaah, the Exalted, blessed him with special wisdom and knowledge of the Deen. His name was Abu Hanifah (rahimullaah) and he is known today as Imam-e-A'dham, the Great Imam and scholar of Islam.

Thank You!

I wanted to thank all of you personally for reading
this book. I hope that it has inspired and motivated you
to take Action Now! There is not a moment to waste to
discover what Life is really about. Please remember that
it is Never too Late to Change and Become the Person You
Want to Be.

Have a Wonderful Journey!

Zohra Sarwari

Have You Booked "The Most Inspirational Muslim Woman Speaker In America"?

Zohra Sarwari

The Ideal Professional Speaker for Your Next Event!

"Zohra Sarwari has a great skill for making you want to achieve on a higher level. Your students will enjoy learning from her!"

Jonathan Sprinkles
Former APCA National College 'Speaker of the Year' www.jsprinkles.com

"After hearing Zohra Sarwari's speech, I was profoundly moved by her enthusiasm to further educate me on the way the Muslim's live. Her knowledge instilled a greater understanding and appreciation in me."

Debbie Burke
High School Teacher
Indianapolis, Indiana

"Zohra Sarwari has stood out as exceptionally creative and extraordinarily passionate about her topics. Her energy is contagious."

Muhammad Alshareef
President, AlMaghrib Institute

"Zohra's effort should be viewed in two disciplines. The first discipline is that we seek a destiny that befits our quality of life. The second discipline is that we seek a destiny to befit the quality of earning in our lives. She has carefully crafted a dialogue of addressing our spiritual, emotional, and financial roadblocks. This book is a win-win for those don't win enough, and for those who may not have won at all. Embrace the book, begin your journey."

Preacher Moss
Founder of "Allah Made me Funny"
The Official Muslim Comedy Tour

"Zohra Sarwari's book is remarkable because it is geared towards not only youth, but all age groups. Anyone who reads this book will take away a valuable lesson filled with inspiration. This book shows us that it does not matter who you are or what your circumstance is, your success lies within you and this book has inspired me to continue with my dreams and turn them into actual goals and pursue them. It doesn't just leave you motivated with no direction, but provides you with actual steps on how to improve yourself and how to achieve your goals with Islamic motivation, something that is lacking these days."

Maida Besic

Interested in other products by Zohra? Take a look at what she has to offer:

'Imagine that Today is Your Last Day'

How would you act if you knew that today was the last day of your life?

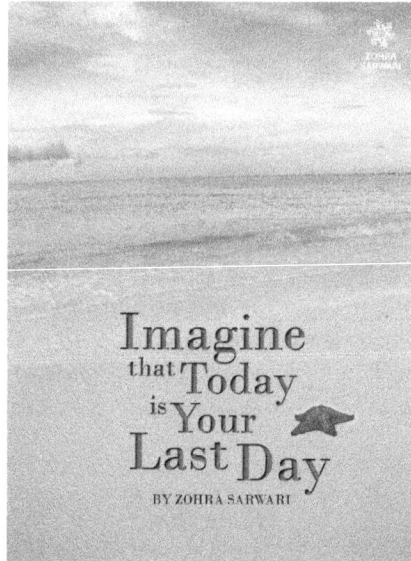

'Imagine that Today is Your Last Day' reveals to you the secrets of living a great life and accepting your fate when it arrives. The book discusses the missing link in your life for which you will have to pay a price after death. Bring every moment to life, it can be your LAST day TODAY! It is an experience that many never think about, let alone go through it.

NO! I AM NOT A TERRORIST!

'Terrorism' and 'terrorist' are the latest media buzzwords! However, do you actually know what each of these terms mean? Do you know who a 'terrorist' is? What comes to your mind when you think of a 'terrorist'? Is it a man with a beard, or is it a woman in a veil? Muslims worldwide are being stereotyped and labeled as 'terrorists'. Have you ever stopped and wondered why? Have you ever made the time to discover what lies under the beard and the dress? Have you ever stopped to think what Islam actually has to say about 'terrorism'? Find the answers to all the above questions and more in this book, **'NO! I AM NOT A TERRORIST!'**

Are Muslim Women Oppressed?
Beyond the Veil

Are Muslim Women
OPPRESSED?

ZOHRA SARWARI

*Learn about the dignified and well-managed lives of Muslim women and know the reasons why they dress the way they do. **'Are Muslim Women OPPRESSED?'** answers your questions: Why do Muslim women wear those weird clothes? Are they doing it for men? Are they inferior? Do they have no rights? **'Are Muslim Women OPPRESSED?'** will reveal the truth behind the concealed Muslim woman. It is a voyage from behind the veil to the real freedom and will give you an insight about Muslim women like you have never read before. Read and clear the misconceptions; separate the facts from the myths!*

Powerful Time Management Skills for Muslims

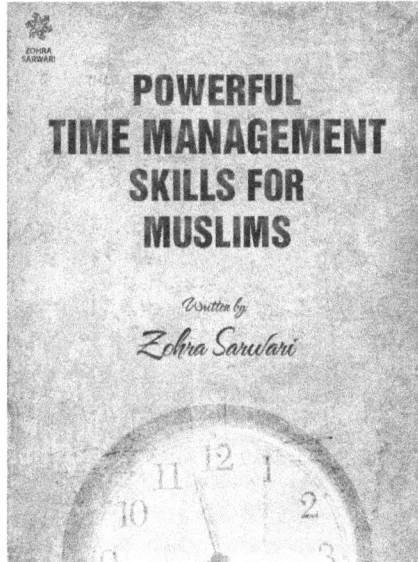

Islam holds Muslims responsible for every action they do and they will be held answerable for the things they are blessed with and how they used it. One of these blessings is 'Time'. **Powerful Time Management Skills for Muslims** *is explaining using references from the Qur'aan and Sunnah how Muslims should live their lives and utilize the precious gift of 'Time'.*

Speaking Skills Every Muslim Must Know

SPEAKING SKILLS
EVERY MUSLIM
MUST KNOW

BY: ZOHRA SARWARI

Confidence is the key to success. **Speaking Skills Every Muslim Must Know** *shares with you some vital methods and techniques to develop confidence and helps you overcome your fear of public speaking. The book guides you following the pattern applied by the Prophet Muhammad (PBUH) and how he delivered his speeches.*

Time Management for Success
(E-book)

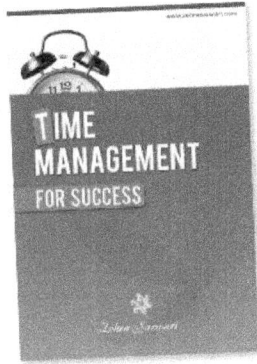

Become a Professional Speaker Today (E-book)

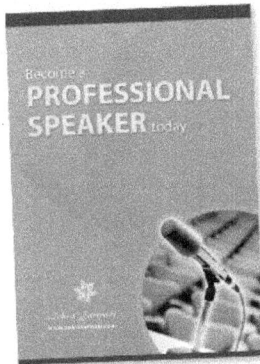

Special Quantity Discount Offer!

- ▶ 20-99 books $13.00 per copy
- ▶ 100-499 books $10.00 each
- ▶ 500-999 books $7.00 each

www.ingramcontent.com/pod-product-compliance
Lightning Source LLC
LaVergne TN
LVHW011400080426
835511LV00005B/367